Preface

This volume contains transcripts of a number of tape-recorded interviews dealing with the late Fleet Admiral Chester W. Nimitz. The people giving the interviews either served with Admiral Nimitz in the U. S. Navy or else knew him in private life. All of the interviews were obtained under the aegis of the Oral History Office in the U. S. Naval Institute during 1969 and 1970. They constitute a part of the on-going project to gather information about the late Fleet Admiral for biographical purposes.

The transcripts were seen by these participants in the Nimitz project and necessary minor corrections were made.

* * * *

Admiral Thomas C. Anderson, MC, USN (Retired)
Mr. James W. Archer
Mr. and Mrs. Edward V. Brewer, Jr.
Mr. George E. Cozard
Captain Tracy D. Cuttle, MC, USN
The Honorable Charles M. Fox, Jr.
Captain George S. Perkins, USNR (Retired)
Rear Admiral Allen G. Quynn, USN (Retired)
Vice Admiral John R. Redman, USN (Retired)

DECLARATION OF TRUST

The undersigned does hereby appoint and designate as his (her) Trustee herein, the Secretary-Treasurer and Publisher of the United States Naval Institute to perform and discharge the following duties, powers, and privileges in connection with the possession and use of a certain taped interview between the undersigned and the Oral History Department of the United States Naval Institute.

(1) As an Open transcript it may be read (or the tape audited) by qualified researchers upon presentation of proper credentials as determined by the Trustee. In the case of interviews about the late Fleet Admiral C. W. Nimitz, it is intended that first use of the material shall be made by the biographer of the Fleet Admiral, Professor E. B. Potter, and the Naval Institute is authorized to deal with the material in this fashion.

(2) It is expressly understood that in giving this authorization, I am in no way precluded from placing such restrictions as I may desire upon use of the interview at any time during my lifetime, nor does this authorization in any way affect my rights to the copyright of any literary expressions that may be contained in the interview.

Witness my hand and seal this 26th day of December 1969.

Thomas C. Anderson

I hereby accept and consent to the foregoing Declaration of Trust and the powers therein conferred upon me as Trustee:

R. E. Bowker Jr.
Secretary-Treasurer and Publisher

Interview with Admiral Thomas C. Anderson,
          MC, USN, Ret.   by Etta Belle Kitchen

Subject: Admiral Nimitz   July 5, 1969

M. Kitchen: I'm awfully happy that you have the time and willingness to discuss your experiences with Admiral Nimitz; and I'm happy to be here.

I know that you did live and shared quarters with Admiral Nimitz during the war in the Pacific. Will you tell me what those dates were?

Admiral Anderson: I arrived in the Pacific at Admiral Nimitz's headquarters in August, 1943. I continued as a member of his staff through the rest of the war in the Pacific. I came home in December, 1945.

Q: Did you go to Guam with him?

Anderson: Yes. When I arrived the headquarters were at Pearl Harbor. Later the headquarters were transferred to Guam, and I went with the part of the staff that was transferred to Guam.

Q: How intimately did you live, and what close contact was your living with Admiral Nimitz?

Anderson - 2

Anderson: We had quarters at Makalapa in Pearl Harbor. I lived in the house with the Admiral. Admiral McMorris, the Chief of Staff, also lived in the house. We three occupied the quarters. From time to time, other officers occupied guests rooms in the house. The permanent residents were Admiral Nimitz, Admiral McMorris, and myself.

Q: How large were the quarters?

Anderson: The quarters had three bedrooms upstairs, and a couple of baths. The Admiral's quarters were downstairs, where he had a suite and a bath.

Q: Can you describe his quarters to me?

Anderson: He had quite a large bedroom, and an ajoining bathroom. There was a hallway that led from the living room back to his quarters. Very modest quarters, I may say - such as any officer on his staff might have occupied. The Admiral was a very disciplined man. It seemed to me that he didn't enjoy many of the privileges of his rank that he could easily have had. He preferred to live like the members of his staff.

Q: How many other rooms were on the first floor?

Anderson: There was a living room - dining room combination. And, of course the kitchen with some quarters for the messmen.

Q: How many messmen did he have?

Anderson: He had, if I remember correctly, the cook and two messmen. In addition to those rooms were the rooms occupied by Admiral Nimitz himself.

Q: The location was on a hill?

Anderson: Yes, the quarters were on a hill at Macalapa above the Naval Station at Pearl Harbor. I think that the Admiral's quarters were probably the highest of all of the quarters located there. I don't know how many quarters were there, but something on the order of 15 or 20 houses in this location.

Q: As a doctor, of course, you were interested in his well-being probably -- certainly his, and all of the other personnel. How did you feel about his health, and what did you do for him?

Anderson: That was a part of my job - to see that the Admiral's health was protected. I may say that he was a man of excellent health. He left very little for the doctor to do. There were two occasions that I recall when he had temporary illness. On one of those occasions, he went to the hospital for a couple of days. He recovered promptly and returned to work. It didn't interfere with his job. In spite of what the doctors could do,

Anderson - 4

there was a stream of people consulting him when he was on his sick bed.

Q: What was the nature of his illness, do you recall?

Anderson: I think probably there's no reason why it shouldn't be disclosed now. He had an acute prostatitis. It responded properly to treatment. For the next year, or more, there was no recurrence of the difficulty.

The second time, he had, what is so common in the tropics, namely gastroenteritis. He didn't go on the sick list at that time, and didn't go to the hospital. But he was examined very carefully, and treated, and recovered while still on active duty.

Those are the only two occasions that I can recall when Admiral Nimitz was not able to be at his desk every day.

Q: What was his reaction to the pressures of which he had an unbelievable amount?

Anderson: He was the calmest man in the face of great problems that I have ever known. He had a very even disposition.

I think when he was younger, he probably had red hair and he had very pale blue eyes. I think he could have a very high temper, but it was under complete control. Regardless of what happened, he spoke quietly and calmly. He never allowed anything to arouse his emotions and so distort his judgement, and

Anderson - 5

his ability to do what should be done.

Q: Did he ever raise his voice, or use profanity?

Anderson: I never heard him speak in anger. I've heard him criticize people very severly; but it was done icely cold and calm, intellectually and not emotionally.

Q: Tell me about some of those. If you can recall any. I think that would be interesting.

Anderson: This was when a severe typhoon occured in the Pacific, and several destroyers were lost. He was convinced that they allowed their fuel tanks to become too low. So, the ships lost their stability.

I heard him express himself - not talk to the officers concerned. He was very severe in his criticism, but it was done quietly as if he were discussing the weather.

Q: As I recall, he wrote a very pointed memorandum to the fleet on the use of seamanship. Am I correct on this? Do you remember something of what that contained?

Anderson: I remember the time, and I remember what he thought about it; yes.

Q: As I recall --- There was some excuse that they were waiting for orders from somebody; and his comments was, that waiting for orders didn't ever overcome the basic knowledge of seamanship which a skipper of a ship should have. Did you ever hear him call down anybody?

Anderson: No, I never heard him call down an officer or anyone.

Q: Did you ever hear him in a situation where he would have humiliated another person?

Anderson: No, I never heard that.

Q: Speaking of his health - what kind of foods did he like?

Anderson: I think we had just a good American diet - meat and potatoes, bread and butter. We ran a good mess, and he had an excellent cook. We all fared well in the Admiral's mess. There were several officers who came to the mess who did not live in the quarters - his aide and several other officers. It always seemed to me, at the table there were people in addition to those that lived in the house, He, also, frequently entertained friends, from Honolulu when the quarters were at Pearl Harbor. Often we had quite a tableful of guests at dinner. He enjoyed having his friends around and I think, obtained much relaxation in that way.

Q: Can you describe an evening with him in his quarters? Either when it was just the three of you, or when he had guests in.

Anderson: The first thing that would happen when we came down to dinner, were cocktails. Inasmuch as I was a medical officer, I was presumed to have some pharmaceutical knowledge and so qualified to mix cocktails. It became my duty to prepare the cocktails. His favorite drink was an old fashioned with a tablespoonful of rum.

Q: You mean added to the bourbon?

Anderson: Added to the bourbon, yes. Following cocktails, we sat down at dinner which was always a very pleasant occasion. The Admiral was a genial man. He made everyone feel at home, and he stimulated conversation. Everybody spoke up, and the dinner was always a pleasant occasion.

Even when things were not going so well following the action at Tarawa, which I think was the low point in the Pacific war, *after my arrival* dinner was not a depressing occasion.

Q: How many cocktails would he have?

Anderson: The Admiral had usually one cocktail. Sometimes if there were a number of guests, he might have a second; but usually one cocktail.

Q: And how about his food - was he a hearty eater?

Anderson: He was a hearty eater. The doctor has no complaint about the Admiral's health and how he took care of himself. His medical officer was a very fortunate individual.

Q: What about his exercising?

Anderson: His chief exercise was walking, and he expected his doctor to accompany him. We would take a walk of two or three miles before breakfast. Breakfast was at 7 o'clock.

Q: Was this every morning?

Anderson: Every morning. After breakfast, we went to the offices; and I didn't see the Admiral again until lunch time. Then we went out for a walk after office hours, and before dinner. This was a long walk. A walk can be real exercise, if you put your vigor into it. And that's the way the Admiral walked. I got to be a pretty good walker before I finished that tour of duty.

Q: You say the morning one was two to three miles. You say the other one was a long walk.

Anderson: There was a favorite place on Guam up on the hill, over looking the harbor. I'm sure that it was 2½ to 3 miles up to the top of the hill. Then the return trip would make it quite a walk.

In addition to that, the Admiral was a great swimmer. I would call him an expert swimmer. Once or twice a week, when the opportunity presented itself, we would make a trip to the beach. He liked ocean swimming, and he would swim far out from shore. I'm not a very good swimmer myself, and I simply had to stay in shallow water; while this older man swam far out in the ocean.

Q: Remarkable, isn't it?

Anderson: He, also enjoyed horseshoe playing. I would say that he was a pretty well-qualified horseshoe player.

Q: That must have come from his early days in Texas.

Anderson: Perhaps.

Q: What about tennis? He played tennis, didn't he?

Anderson: No, I did not see him play tennis.

Q: I've also heard reference to a pistol-shooting range that he would have near his office.

Anderson: I can't give you any opinion about that. I do not know.

Q: He has quite a reputation of being quite a story-teller. I've heard people say that, but I can't find anyone who can remember any of his stories.

Anderson: He was a story-teller, and he liked to hear stories. I can't recall stories now. Some of them perhaps would best not be recorded, but they were good stories.

Q: On this recording thing -- I sometimes think that stories a man tells, or how he relaxes; you might be able to evaluate the man as a human. I've heard it said that he was a story-teller and that he had a good sense of humor; but I am searching for someone who can tell me some of his stories.

Anderson: I can tell you a story. It was one that I told, although it was not original with me. On occasion, particularly if they had guests, the Admiral would call on me as his raconteur. The story goes something like this --

The man was a patient at an Institution. He came up for parole, and the board asked him questions, and were about to conclude that he was qualified for parole. But there was one man on the board who wasn't satisfied. He said he'd like to ask this man another question.

So he asked the man, "When you get out of this Institution, what's the first thing you're going to do?" The man said, he had a girl, and he was going to see her and they would go out to dinner. Then after dinner, they would go to a show. And he was going to have the first good time that he'd had for a long time. The board said, "The man sounds entirely normal, and let's grant him his parole."

This one member said, "I'M not quite satisfied. I'd like to ask the man another question." So he asked him, "After the show, what are you going to do then?" The man was a little embarrassed, and hesitant in his answer. But he finally said, "My girl and I are going to go up to her room." The board said, "That's enough, the man's entirely normal. Let's give him his parole."

This fellow said, "Wait a minute, I'm not satisfied." "After you get up to the girl's room, what are you going to do then?" The man said, "She's going to sit on my lap, and we're going to neck a little bit." The board said, "Enough, enough, let the man go."

But this one man said, "Wait a minute. I'm not quite satisfied." "What are you going to do then?" The patient was considerably embarrassed, and hesitant; but he finally said, "I'm going to feel of her silken ankle." The board said, "Wait a minute, let's not go any farther."

The man said, "Wait a minute, one more question." "What are you going to do then?" The patient said, "When I get up to her garter, I'm going to take it and make myself a slingshot. And I'm coming back to this place, and break every window in the building."

That's the story.

Q: It's delightful, isn't it? Then did he take your story and tell it himself on occasion?

Anderson: I never heard him tell it, he always had me tell it.

Q: You tell it very well, I can understand why he did. That's very delightful. If you think of any of his other stories when you have the tape back, don't hesitate to add them. I think for a biographer that would be a delightful experience to see these things as human being.

Anderson: I remember on one occasion when the Admiral had made a trip back to Washington. I believe that he had seen Prime Minister Churchill in Washington, if I remember correctly. At any rate, when he returned; he had one of the Prime Minister's cigars.

At that time, I smoked cigars. I have long since quit the habit, but I did smoke cigars. When the Admiral returned, he gave me Mr. Churchill's cigar. He said, "Doctor, save this cigar, and smoke it on some special occasion."

The occasion came, when he had a tableful of guests one evening. After the dinner, when we were still at the table, he said, "Doctor, I think this is the special occasion when you should smoke the Prime Minister's cigar." So, he told the people about the cigar. I had to excuse myself, and go and get the cigar. It was an enormous affair, and very dark in color. I was accustomed to smoking cigars, and I lit the cigar with all attention focused on me. Everything went very well for awhile. But, as the Admiral tells it, the doctor said, "Gee, it's getting hot around here." I wiped the perspiration from my forehead, and finally I had to excuse myself. It was a very strong cigar, and very embarrassing to me.

Q: Oh, I bet it was. Did he feel bad because he'd embarrassed you?

Anderson: No, he thought it was a good joke.

Q: He didn't mind a joke then at your expense.

Anderson: Not at all.

Q: I guess you didn't finish the cigar.

Anderson: I did not.

Anderson - 14

Q: Did he have a favorite dinner that he liked?

Anderson: I can't recall about that. The one thing that I recall about the mess is that we had very good food.

Q: You told me a little bit about how he reacted to battle loses and reports that came in. Can you elaborate a little bit more on how you felt that he threw off the tensions, if he did when he left his office?

Anderson: After I arrived there, the battle of Tarawa was the most serious action. We were successful at Tarawa, but it came at great expense. I think before I got there, the battle of Midway was a more serious action.

When the news of the battle came back at the headquarters, the message was, "The result is in doubt." This came one evening, and I could see that the Admiral was very deeply disturbed. He said, "I've sent in there everything we had, and it's plenty. I don't see why we shouldn't succeed." And of course, they did succeed. But it was at terrific loss.

Q: How did he display his concern? Did he walk up and down?

Anderson: No, he was sitting in his chair. I knew that he was disturbed. He didn't appear excited, and he didn't walk up and down. He just was speaking his thoughts, and those were his thoughts.

Q: How was his facial expression?

Anderson: Just calm and cool as if he were drinking an cocktail.

Q: It would have been, what, then, his tone of voice; and the words he chose?

Anderson: The words he said, yes.

Q: I wonder if you were able to observe if he was a letter writer - a personal letter writer?

Anderson: Yes, I think he was. I don't know very much about it because many of the letters he dictated in his office, and the more personal ones he wrote in longhand in his room. I do not have firsthand knowledge about that.

Q: Did you ever happen to receive a letter from him?

Anderson: Yes. It was a telephone message that we had. He lived in Berkeley for several years after he retired, and we called on him at his home in Berkeley. Then, towards the end, he lived in quarters on Yerba Buena Island. We were at the quarters there once. We had Christmas letters, we always had Christmas letters.

Anderson - 16

Q: Written in longhand?

Anderson: Yes.

Q: Do you have any of those?

Anderson: No, I have not.

Q: Did you feel the warmth of the man? I know you spoke of his being extremely congenial. Could you speak on that point?

Anderson: He was a very good ship mate - a quiet retiring man, soft-spoken, very friendly; but he was the boss. And no one ever forgot it.

Q: Did you ever feel like taking any liberties with him?

Anderson: No, I never did.

Q: I mean, not you, would one?

Anderson: No, no. For myself, I just had the greatest respect for him. I think that he was the finest naval officer that I have ever known. He was a *Real Officer*!

I think the reaction generally - no one would take any liberties with Admiral Nimitz. What he said, went; and that was it.

Q: I think I said to you before that I had heard it quoted that - no criticism of him by anyone had ever been said.

Anderson: I think that's correct.

Q: It's incredible, isn't it? Did he speak of his family?

Anderson: Oh, yes, particularly the children. On one occasion when I came back to the states, he sent green coffee beans to the two girls. I called on them; they lived in Washington at the time. He often refered to his family - his wife, daughters, also his son.

Q: Did he have their pictures displayed in his room?

Anderson: Yes, their pictures were there.

Q: What kind of clothing did he wear around the quarters?

Anderson: He was very meticulous about his uniform. Of course, we wore khaki. His uniform was always in perfect order. For the hiking, as I recall, he unbuttoned his shirt at the throat. He wore his uniform when he hiked. Without the insignia, he was just a hiker.

Anderson - 18

Q: In the tropics, he didn't have his blouse on, he would just wear the shirt?

Anderson: Yes, they had the insignia on the collar. I can't be too sure about that, but I don't believe he wore his insignia when we went out for a hike.

Q: Did he wear pajamas, did he wear a bathrobe? Did you ever see him when he was ready for bed?

Anderson: Oh, yes. He often wore pajamas and a bathrobe. He was fond of music. He had a record player in the living room. He liked classical music. After dinner he'd come out and listen to music for an hour or more. Usually he was in his bathrobe.

Q: Had he selected these records himself?

Anderson: Yes, many of them he had selected. And many of them were given to him.

Q: Do you remember any of his favorite recordings?

Anderson: Brahms, he had a picture of Brahms. He liked his music very much. I'm not very much of a musician myself, so I don't remember too well.

Q: Generally classical music?

Anderson: Yes, in general, classical music.

Q: Did he have any objection to modern music?

Anderson: I never heard him express any.

Q: What was his bathrobe like? That's a tough one?

Anderson: I can't remember about that, informal dress.

Q: I was wondering if it wasn't a navy-issue bathrobe.

Anderson: No.

Q: Did you ever hear him use profanity?

Anderson: Never.

Q: Even if he got mad?

Anderson: Never.

Q: Never. Do you know anything about whether he was a religious man, or not?

Anderson: I can't answer that question, I don't know. ~~So far as~~ I know, we ~~did not~~ went go to church. on a number of occasions but the opportunity did not present itself often.

Q: Did you ever hear him express his philosophy of life?

Anderson: No, I can't say that I did. His way of expressing his philosophy was to go to work. And he expressed his philosophy very well. He was a very conscientious employee of the Navy.

Q: That may be a philosophy of itself.

Anderson: I think so.

Q: Did you ever have the feeling that he had any doubts as to the outcome of his job?

Anderson: Never, he was sure he would win.

Q: I'm sure if anyone of us starts a job, and we don't think we're going to do it, it's almost like taking a trip - if you don't think you're going to get there, you don't start.

Did he ever play Bridge?

Anderson: Oh, yes, good Bridge player.

Q: Did you ever play with him?

Anderson: No, I'm not a Bridge player. He also liked to play Poker.

Q: These are interesting things, that I love to hear you remember.

Anderson: And he was a very good Poker player. I played Poker with him, to my distress.

Q: Tell me about that.

Anderson: Just a nice friendly poker game, where I didn't win.

Q: Do you remember how much he won?

Anderson: In general, he was successful. He did that like he did everything else - very thoroughly and very carefully.

Q: And he was a winner at these Poker games?

Anderson: Usually, yes.

Q: Did he ever put any limits on the stakes?

Anderson - 22

Anderson: Oh, it was a very small game. It was fun, very enjoyable.

Q: Who all would play with him?

Anderson: He had friends in Honolulu. There was a family - the H. Alexander Walker's - they were great friends of his. He frequently went to their house for an evening of relaxation. There were several civilian friends of the Walkers that used to be there. He had many invitations to places in Honolulu, and he refused them all. He just couldn't answer all the calls. So, he solved the difficulty by having the particular friends - the Walkers - where he went for a little relaxation. His job was so demanding, that he simply couldn't give much time to social activities.

Q: What time did he get up in the morning?

Anderson: He got up about six o'clock in the morning.

Q: What time did he usually go to bed? If there was a usual?

Anderson: He went down to the office always in the evening, and looked over all the dispatches. I think he got to bed by 10:30 or 11 o'clock at night.

Q: What about his Bridge? Do you know who his Bridge partners might be?

Anderson: No, I can't recall. I can't answer that question.

Q: Did he like the movies?

Anderson: So far as I know, he never went to the movies.

Q: All the time he was out there, there were no families - at least of the Naval Officer.

Anderson: No, no families, that's true.

Q: Tell me about the move to Guam. If that changed any of his procedures, or his way of living.

Anderson: I think about half the staff went out to Guam. It went off very smoothly, and very quickly. After Guam was taken, the public works people got out there. The headquarters buildings were put up with room for the staff. We went out by plane; I flew out with the Admiral. His quarters were ready, and his office was ready. There was no interruption to the routine of his work.

Anderson - 24

Q: Was Guam, as far as the temperature is concerned - it's north of Honolulu - was it unpleasant?

Anderson: No, I didn't find it so - tropical. It was warm; but the tropics in general, as I found them, are not as hot as Washington and Philadelphia in the summertime. No, Guam was not unpleasant, as far as climate is concerned.

Q: What was his weight as a rule?

Anderson: I should know that - I think he ran somewhere around 160 - 165 pounds. I think he was about six feet tall, maybe a little over.

Q: He was right for his height.

Anderson: Yes, he was. He was not overweight at all; he kept himself in excellent condition. He didn't hardly need a doctor. He took care of himself.

His health record would tell exactly. Maybe my figures aren't correct, I'm not too sure. It's 25 years now since all this went on.

Q: Let me just ask an overall question. You've told me how you felt towards him as a Naval Officer. How do you feel about him as a person?

Anderson: Oh, he was a fine fellow, you bet. He was a fine man.

Q: If a man could love another one, would you say you loved him?

Anderson: I would think so, yes.

Q: And I think men do love others, as properly.

Anderson: Perhaps. I certainly feel the very highest regard for him, and respect. He was a very competent man, and a fair shooter. You couldn't ask for a better shipmate.

Q: That has so many implications of fineness. It's about as good a compliment as you can give another person.

Anderson: I couldn't say too much in that regard. This man is my ideal of what a Naval Officer should be.

Q: I've heard him described as a great man. How do you feel as to that?

Anderson: I guess he was. But so far as I'm concerned; he was just an A number one shipmate, and a good friend.

Anderson - 26

Q: That is the first time that you've used that word. Did you realize that? You say he's a good friend. That gives a feeling of warmth, I think.

Anderson: Yes, that's true.

Q: And you saw him after both of you had retired?

Anderson: Yes. He lived in Berkeley for several years. Whenever we were in the San Francisco Bay area, we always went over to call on them.

When they finally moved over to quarters on Yerba Buena Island, he insisted we stay with them. We were there one night and had dinner with them. Played horseshoes with him, and had cocktails with him. Really had a very delightful evening.

Q: Could you feel a change in his personality - having left the terrible burdens which he had carried through the years?

Anderson: Yes, I think so. Also, the last time that I saw him, the Admiral was getting older. He was the same kindly, genial personality as always. Not quite as aggressive, not quite as firm in his attitute; but the same man.

Q: Did he ever have a nickname that you know of?

Anderson - 27

Anderson: Not that I know of. Everybody called him Admiral Nimitz.

Q: I've heard that said - that even among Admirals, it was always Admiral. Sometimes people have nicknames that you don't use to their face.

I can understand why Mrs. Nimitz thought you would be souce of information about the Admiral.

Anderson: Of course, when you live with a person a couple of years, you become quite well acquainted; and learn about them.

Q: Strangely enough, the characteristics that you speak of, even as intimately as you lived, are almost the characteristics and traits that one has heard from him in his professional life.

Anderson: Yes, I think that's true.

Q: Do you have any other anecdotes that you can remember? I love the one about the cigar.

Anderson: No, my memory grows a little dim. It's a long time.

Q: How did he greet you? Do you remember, when you first came aboard?

Anderson - 28

Anderson: Andy. Many people call me Andy, on account of my last name. He always called me Andy.

Q: Did he know you before you came out?

Anderson: Yes. He was skipper of the destroyer base here in San Diego before they had a naval station. I was the surgeon at the naval hospital. We became acquainted with the Nimitz's then. We had a daughter about the age of the Nimitz's son. They used to go around together some in San Diego. And that's when we first got acquainted with the Nimitz's.

Q: Did he seem glad to see you when you came out to Pearl Harbor

Anderson: Oh, yes. I felt it a great compliment to me when Jondreau was lost that he selected me to come out as his surgeon.

Q: That brings up a point in that he did select his officers.

Anderson: I don't know about that. But I think there's no question of that Admiral Nimitz selected the officers he wanted on his staff.

Q: Did you ever see him put his arms around anyone, or put his hand on their shoulder, or any personal contact?

Anderson: I've seen him shake hands with many people, but I never saw him show any signs of that kind. I think that he had favorites all right that he thought a great deal of. He was a retiring type of man, he was a soft-spoken Texan; not a fellow that beat people over their heads or slapped them on the back. He just shook hands and spoke to them very quietly.

Q: How did he indicate that he had favorites?

Anderson: By not indicating to them that he didn't like the way they were performing their duty.

Q: I know that these nuances that I'm asking you are difficult, but when I try to ask you questions, I think to myself -- if I'm reading about Admiral Nimitz, what would I like to know about him as a human being? That's why I am asking this type of question.

Anderson: Yes. It's very difficult for the average person to describe the character of his friends. He can say a few things, but it's not easy. Your questions help a great deal in saying what I thought about him.

Q: If they are helpful, I'm glad. I don't mean to be pushing you to extreme.

Did you know Admiral Nimitz, Mrs. Anderson? I'm sure you did, you met them here, didn't you? I'd love to have your reactions toward the Admiral; your thoughts about him. I'd love to have your comment.

Mrs. Anderson: I have the feeling that my husband didn't make Admiral Nimitz appear quite as warm as he was.

Q: Of course, that may be the difference between men and men; and a woman and man. I mean a woman's reaction to him. Tell me more about that, I'd love to hear you say more.

Mrs. Anderson: I think he was reserved and quiet and very dignified; but he had a great warmth too. He loved people, and he showed it.

Q: How did he treat ladies? Women? Girls?

Mrs. Anderson: I don't know that I know that?

Q: I mean, how did he act to you? Did he kiss you when he saw you? Or would he put his arms around you?

Mrs. Anderson: I think not.

Q: Neither of those? Would he shake hands?

Anderson - 31

Mrs. Anderson: Oh, yes, he would shake hands.

Q: Call you by your first name?

Mrs. Anderson: Yes, always.

Anderson: He was very popular with the ladies out at the quarters in Pearl Harbor. Of course, whenever the Admiral invited couples to dinner; they always came, quite happily. It just seemed to me that the ladies particularly enjoyed the evening. He was a royal host.

Q: Did he like the ladies to dress up?

Anderson: Oh, yes. He liked a nice dinner, he liked it very much.

Q: I regret, so much, that I was never able to meet him. Do you know how he felt about the WAVES?

Anderson: I think that he was cordial towards the WAVES. We didn't have many out there. There were women. The Red Cross had representatives. Were there WAVES out there? Yes, there were.

Q: Winny Quick was there, and she married Admiral Collins. And Billy Wild; I think both of them were out there.

Did you ever hear him express his opinion about women in the Navy?

Anderson: No, I can't recall now.

Q: Did he ever invite nurses or WAVES to his quarters?

Anderson: Yes, we had nurses at his quarters. In Guam, I remember particularly. The nurses out there had isolated duty, and I think he took pains to have the girls up at his quarters on several occasions. We had nurses at dinner.

Q: I want you to feel free to say any other comments that come to your mind.

Anderson: As I said, I don't think of anything further. I've tried to express my idea, and it's a little difficult for an ordinary layman to put into words - especially when so much time has passed. Many things that happened I'm sure that I no longer remember. Time dims your memories.

Q: I agree with that, but I don't agree with ordinary layman as applied to yourself.

Anderson: I'm not a writer or a speaker. My business has been in other directions.

Q: I think you've given a lot of detail that I doubt would be available from anyone else.

Anderson: I'm very happy if it's helpful at all.

Q: I'M sure that it is. I'm sure Mrs. Nimitz will enjoy hearing your comments about the Admiral. I hope that they will be able to find a biographer who will do justice to him as a human being.

Mrs. Anderson, anything more? I hope that you're not having any thoughts that you're holding back,;because your comments, I think, are invaluable.

Anderson: My wife is the smartest one, she can really express herself well.

Q: No, I didn't know that. I wish you'd come over and tell me -- you've been, I know, with the Nimitz's socially?

Mrs. Anderson: Not too much.

Q: You were in their quarters, were you?

Mrs. Anderson: Oh, yes.

Q: Can you describe the Admiral and Mrs. Nimitz - or an evening with them?

Mrs. Anderson: They had a very interesting home filled with mememtoes from their long life, and their many travels. We especially enjoyed the evening we spent with them on Yerba Buena.

Q: Yerba Buena means goat island, doesn't it?

Anderson: Goat Island is the place.

Mrs. Anderson: It was a very handsome large old white house. They seemed especially to be at home in it.

Q: Did he take you around and show you all of his mememtoes?

Mrs. Anderson: I don't remember that he did that time, but at different times he did show us a good many things. He had a very very large library. He told us then - that was the last time we were there, it was within a year of his death,

I think - that publishers were sending him books almost daily. As new books came out, they were being sent to the Admiral as gifts.

Q: Related to him, necessarily?

Mrs. Anderson: No, not necessarily. Books of all sorts. So, his library had grown just in the last years of his life.

Q: That was one thing I meant to ask you, Admiral Anderson. As to what he read - did he have time to do any reading?

Anderson: Yes, he did, he read at night - after he retired. Another thing he did - he'd wake up in the night, he'd tell me about it. Something would occur to him, and he'd write it down because things like that that come to you in the night - the next morning you can't remember what it was. Things in regard to the progress of the war in the Pacific. Things on his mind - he'd wake up in the night, the idea would occur to him, and he'd write it down; in order to go over it again the next day.

Yes, he was a reader. He read at night a good deal after he turned in. He would read in the evening.

Q: Do you know whether he read detective stories, or history, or biographies?

Anderson: No, his reading was more serious. He read history particularly. He was a great history man, and biographies and so forth - that type of literature.

Q: I wonder if he slept well?

Anderson: Yes, he did. He was a good sleeper. Never had any complaint about that. I never gave the Admiral a sleeping pill all the time I was with him.

Q: Nor a tranquilizer, I imagine.

Anderson: Nor a tranquilizer. And boy, he had occasion to have them, too.

Q: I know, I don't understand how the man could carry the weight he carried. I really don't.

Mrs. Anderson, if you have any further comments, I'd love to hear them. You think you've said everything, and then something brings up something else. And the next thing you know, you wish I'd said that.

Anderson: One other thing that occurs to me now is the Admiral's knowledge of what was going on out there, and his comphrension of the situation. It was brought to my attention in this way - Dr. Leahy, a surgeon from Boston, visited the headquarters. I think it was at Pearl Harbor. He saw the Admiral in his office. How much time he spent down there, I don't know. But Leahy himself was a very competent person - long since passed away.

I talked to him later, and he was astounded at the Admiral's grasp and comphrension, and knowledge of details of what was going on in the area. The Pacific Ocean is a great place, and there were a lot of people out there, and a lot of ships.

Leahy was just astounded at the information that the Admiral could give him about the situation in the Pacific.

Q: Did he like to fly, do you know?

Anderson: I think that he did. He flew everywhere. We visited all of the areas of action; just as soon as they had a landing field established ashore, the Admiral flew right out there.

Q: I was wondering about that.

Anderson: He always went by plane. He took me along. I had the privilege of visiting all of the islands that were taken in the Central Pacific. And he went by plane, and I think he enjoyed flying.

Q: I'm sure you have mememtoes, or pictures, or things of that nature.

Anderson: Surprisingly little, for ~~some~~ good reason. There was such a black-out on any record of what you were doing, that I didn't try to make any record. I came home, I think, with most of my experiences just in my head and not in my hands.

Q: And were you in Tokyo Bay with him?

Anderson: No, I did not go to Tokyo Bay. There was a great demand for space on the plane that the Admiral took to Tokyo Bay at the time of the surrender. To be frank about it, I didn't even ask. The reason that I didn't ask, was that I knew that the Admiral was just overwhelmed with the requests. He had to pick among high-ranking officers.

Mrs. Anderson: Have you seen that?

Q: No. That's a lovely picture.

Mrs. Anderson: That appeared in LIFE magazine.

Q: Tell me about this picture, and I'm going to describe it.
Admiral Nimitz is seated in walking-shorts, three-quarter length socks, and an open khaki shirt; and he's wearing his insignia here. He looks like a youthful man. He has four officers seated on the divan on one side, and two officers on the other; and another officer standing behind him.

I hate to say it — I have to ask which one is you? I would have recognized it, but your face is turned away.

Where is this picture taken, Admiral?

Anderson: That was taken on Guam. That was on the porch of the Admiral's quarters at Guam.

Q: Do you have another copy of this?

Anderson: No, I think not. That's the only one we have.

Q: When you want to think of who you would like to give it to -- the Naval Institute would love to have it.

Mrs. Anderson: I'm sure there are plenty of copies of this. I saw it in LIFE during the war, and then later we had this.

Q: They perhaps have a copy of it in the Naval Historical.

Mrs. Anderson, I think the comment you made about Admiral Nimitz; when I told Admiral Anderson if there were any things which he didn't want to have disclosed until sometime in the future -- just repeat the comment that you made. Do you remember what you said? Can you say it again, because you said it beautifully?

Mrs. Anderson: I don't even remember what I said.

Anderson: Well, it's true just the same. I think that Admiral Nimitz's life was an open book.

Q: That was it.

Anderson: Anybody can read it, and it will be very pleasant reading.

Q: That was what Mrs. Anderson implied. That there was nothing that anyone might know about him that ---

Anderson: You know, when you live with a man, you know pretty well what he's about.

Mrs. Anderson: Here's a very late picture of the Admiral, taken in the yard of their home in Berkeley.

Q: Isn't that something to treasure? Isn't that beautiful? How old was he when he died?

Anderson: He was in his early 80s. He was about two years older than I.

Q: Look at all that gold. Marvelous face. You look not unalike. You are less lined than he, but don't you think there's a certain shape of the face ---

Mrs. Anderson: No, there really wasn't - not a resemblance.

Q: That's a gorgeous picture. He, to me, was legendary. I couldn't believe that he was real.

Mrs. Anderson: He was real, he was a real man.

This section of a radio broadcast came each morning from Guam, and one morning the broadcaster said, "This is Guam (he told the time, 8 o'clock in the morning). We've just had callers; Admiral Nimitz and his medical officer have just been here to inspect the station."

Q: My, that was a thrill for you to hear, wasn't it? At least, you knew he was all right then.

Mrs. Anderson: I knew that day that he was alive.

Q: Isn't that a beautiful picture?

Mrs. Anderson: This is much more formal, but I think that other one is just a beautiful picture.

Anderson - 42

Q: This is earlier, I think.

Mrs. Anderson: Yes.

Q: I'm looking at photographs that the Andersons have been given by Admiral Nimitz.
This one makes him an extremely handsome man.

Anderson: He was a good looking man.

Mrs. Anderson: He was tall, straight up and very erect, very military.

Q: Did you think he was handsome? Would you consider him handsome?

Anderson: You bet he's handsome. He had white hair, ruddy face, pale blue eyes - he was a good looking man.

Q: He scared me so, because of his position that I --

Anderson: He gave me the Legion of Merit.

Q: Isn't that lovely.

Anderson: That was a very proud moment when he pinned the medal on.

Q: I'm looking at the picture with Admiral Nimitz pinning the Legion of Merit on Admiral Anderson.
You don't have anything to complain about in looks.

Anderson: Me?

Q: Oh, my, those are really treasures.

Anderson: Yes, they are.

Q: If you can think of anything else, I'd just love to stay and talk.

Mrs. Anderson: It may be that if we had given it a little more thought, we could have expressed ourselves a little better. Just on the spur of the moment, it's a little hard to remember things.

Q: I think a free rejoiner, as we've had, is rather better than a study thing. With this tape coming back to you, you will think of things, I'm sure. Maybe tonight, in the middle of the night, you can get up and make a note about a story. Then when it comes back to you, feel free to edit it or add, or whatever you like.

Anderson: I don't think of anything further right now.

Q: Admiral and Mrs. Anderson, this has been delightful for me.

Anderson - 44

Anderson: We're very happy that you came. I like to talk about the Admiral. It's no work for us at all.

Q: You speak of him very well.

Anderson: I liked him very much.

Q: I'm sure you did. You maybe loved him?

Anderson: Yes, I guess so.

Q: I guess it's a word that men don't often times use about another one, but I think it is a properly useful one in certain circumstances. Thank you, sir.

INDEX

for an interview

with

ADMIRAL THOMAS C. ANDERSON, U. S. NAVY (RET.)

Athletics and exercises, 8-9

Berkeley, 15, 26, 40

Brahms, 18

Churchill, Prime Minister Winston, 12

Collins, RADM Howard L., 32

Collins, Winnifred Quick, 32

Disposition, 4-6

Guam, 1, 9, 23-24, 32, 39

Illnesses, 3-4

Jondreau, Romeo Joseph, 28

Leahy, Dr., 36-37

Legion of Merit, 42-43

<u>Life</u>, 38-39

Makalapa, 2-3

McMorris, Admiral Charles H., 2

Midway, Battle of, 14

Nimitz, Mrs. Chester W., 34

Pearl Harbor, 1-3, 6, 28, 31, 36

Stories, 10-12

Tarawa, 7, 14

Tokyo Bay, 38

Walker, H. Alexander family, 22

WAVES, 31-32

Wilde, CAPT Louise, 32

Yerba Buena Island, 15, 26, 34

DECLARATION OF TRUST

The undersigned does hereby appoint and designate as his (or her) Trustee herein, the Secretary-Treasurer and Publisher of the United States Naval Institute to perform and discharge the following duties, powers, and privileges in connection with the possession and use of a certain taped interview between the undersigned and the Oral History Department of the United States Naval Institute.

(1) As an Open transcript. It may be read (or the tape audited) by qualified researchers upon presentation of proper credentials as determined by the Trustee.

(2) It is expressly understood that in giving this authorization, I am in no way precluded from placing such restrictions as I may desire upon use of the interview at any time during my lifetime, nor does this authorization in any way affect my rights to the copyright of any literary expressions that may be contained in the interview.

Witness my hand and seal this 2 day of November 1969:

James W. Archer

I hereby accept and consent to the foregoing Declaration of Trust and the powers therein conferred upon me as Trustee:

R. E. Bowker Jr.
Secretary-Treasurer and Publisher

- 1 -

Interview with James W. Archer   by Etta-Belle Kitchen
La Jolla, California   August 2, 1969
Subject: Admiral Nimitz

Commander Kitchen: Good afternoon Mr. Archer. I'm glad to be here.

Mr. Archer: I'm very glad to have you here Commander Kitchen. It's a priviledge and pleasure to be interviewed by you.

Q: I'm sure that anyone who knew Admiral Nimitz, at least it's been my experience, any one who did know him, loves to talk about him. To begin with, why don't you tell me about your contact, how you happened to have contact with Admiral Nimitz?

Archyer: My first meeting with Admiral Nimitz was early in the month of August 1926. We met in front of Old North Hall on the Berkeley campus of the University of California. I was walking across the campus as an extremely green freshman. I was greeted by the Admiral, then of course a young Captain. I believe a rather junior Captain. He inquired if I might be interested in enrolling in the first class of a program in Naval Science and Tactics.

Archer - 2

Q: Did you know who he was then?

Archer: No.

Q: Was he in uniform?

Archer: Yes. I informed him that I would be interested, but I did not know if it would be appropriate as my father was an Army Colonel. That seemed to bemuse Captain Nimitz. Very shortly thereafter, less than an hour, I was enrolled.

Q: Did he make any preamble, or introduce himself? He just simply came up to you and made this comment?

Archer: I was just passing by the entrance to the Old North Hall. He was standing there, called me over, and inquired if I'd be interested.

Q: Did he ask who you were, where you were from, anything at all?

Archer: No, not that I recall.

Q: How many were in the group at that time, do you know?

Archer: They were just commencing enrolling people, and it's my recollection that he enrolled 120; but he insisted later that it was 150.

Q: Were you the first one enrolled, perhaps?

Archer: I believe I was one of the first.

Q: Let's say you were the first. If nobody knows the difference, you might as well be the first.

Archer: I could have been the first. Thereafter, I importuned my life long friend, and fraternity brother-- we were fraternity brothers both in high school and college-- and my roommate; now Captain Tracy D. Cuttle, Commanding Officer of the Naval Hospital at Chelsea, Massachusetts; to enroll with me.

Thereafter Captain Nimitz and his Executive Officer, Commander Ernest L. Gunther - who incidentally later became Commander of all the Air Forces in the Pacific, and whom I called upon in Guam in 1944 or 45 - challenged Tracy Cuttle and me to handball matches. It is my recollection that we played once a week for the three years that they were stationed at Berkeley. Although they were spotting us approximately 30 years in age by way of handicap, I do not recall that we two Cadets ever won two out of three games against those senior

Archer - 4

officers.

Q: Admiral Nimitz all his life, was almost a fanatic for physical fitness. So, apparently he started very early on that regime.

Archer: Admiral Nimitz, then of course Captain, particularly seemed to enjoy teaching us how to play the game; but continuously beat us. As you indicated, and I believe every one knows; Admiral Nimitz was always a great athlete and a great advocate of physical fitness.

Captain Nimitz strove very hard to make real Naval Officers out of our group. Being the first unit, they obviously wanted it to be outstanding if possible. However, due to basic deficiencies in some of our high school trainings; particularly in mathematics, which I will elude to later, some of us had a very difficult time with the courses in navigation and engineering. Navigation proved to be a nightmare for me.

Q: I wanted to ask you, unless you had planned to discuss it later - what naval courses you took? Besides navigation.

Archer: Engineering, Naval tactics, we made a great study of famous naval battles, naval history. I would actually have to look at my file, to give that to you very accurately; I can't recall. But it was a course designed as closely as possible to the course at Annapolis. Having in mind the fact that we had to take other undergraduate liberal arts, or engineerying, or pre-med courses.

Q: How many hours a week did you spend in your naval courses?

Archer: I think a mimimum of ten hours a week.

Q: Plus your undergraduate work?

Archuer: Yes.

Q: That was extremely heavy, wasn't it?

Archer: It was a heavy course. It was designed to be heavy. As I said, they wanted to make us as closely comparable to a Naval Academy graduate as they could. Recognizing that some of the young men were going to go into specialities. Like I had in mind even at that time, law. Captain Cuttle was in pre-med. Captain Chase, who I will mentioned later, was in engineering.

So, our naval courses had to, in some degree, coincide with our other undergraduate courses. We all took drilling, seamanship, I neglected to mention, and small boat handling and gunnery. We would drill at least three times a week. We had gunnery practice; we would fire small arms and three inch guns. We fired on the rifle range very frequently. We were required to qualify with a Colt 45 automatic and with a rifle.

Q: And how much contact with these courses did Captain Nimitz have?

Archer: He was very much in charge in supervision.

Q: How many professors did they have teaching the naval courses, or do you recall?

Archer: I would say there were about six commissioned officers -- Captain Nimitz, Commander Gunther, Commander Murphy, a Lieutenant Commander whose name I don't recall, and a couple more junior men -- and about six non-commissioned officers.

Q: Did you enjoy it?

Archer: Very much.

Q: What were the benefits you received in a monetary way?

Archer: Nothing in those days. That was long before they started giving any scholarships or any monetary assistance

Archer - 7

at all.

Q: You got nothing at all financially?

Archer: We were furnished our uniform, but no money whatsoever. In fact, I think, when we went on summer cruises; they were finally able to get an appropriation to give us a dollar a day, for two or three weeks summer cruises.

Q: What was your motivation then in participating in NROTC?

Archer: Just interested in it. It was a Very good course.

Q: Interest seems to fail these days, at least based on what one reads in the paper. Maybe the newspapers aren't accurate.

Archer: I don't think there's as little interest in the ROTC courses as you read in the papers. I'll come to that later. When I succeeded Admiral Nimitz on the Board of Regents of the University of California, He importuned us repeatedly to maintain the ROTC program, and I naturally was a great advocate of doing so.

Q: I don't want to interrupt you, but I do like to have you speak freely on any of these subjects.

Archer: As I indicated, I had very great difficulties in mastering navigation because of my poor basic mathematical training; of which Admiral Nimitz reminded me as late as 1958 when we were founding the new branch of the University of California in San Diego. What a great need there is for better mathematics. He repeatedly alluded to

Q: Was he referring to your lack of preparation?

Archer: He alluded specifically to that - my lack of preparation. He had never forgotten that.

Q: I've heard stories - little incidents of that nature to which he made reference time and again, many many years later. He had a fantastic recollection for an individuals personal characteristics.

Archer: He certainly could remember my struggling through navigation in 1926, 27, and 29, thirty years later.

He permitted me to hand in one of my final examinations in navigation, after I'd been working on it from about nine o'clock one morning until five a.m. the next morning. We used to joke about where the ship would have been on the beach by that time. It had taken me that length of time to figure out where we were.

Q: You worked on it for how long?

Archer: From 9 a.m. until 5 a.m. the next morning.

Q: Where was he all this time?

Archer: The instructors had long gone, and closed the building.

Q: Letting you stay by yourself working out your problems.

Archer: Yes.

Q: I hope he gave you a passing mark after all that effort.

Archer: I think I passed, but I'm sure it was not with honors.

Our class suffered a very heavy mortality due principally to the stock market crash and the depression of '29 and '30. I believe, and I'm pretty sure of this figure, that there were only 21 in the original group that graduated. We were commissioned in June of 1930.

Going back to some of the interesting occasions with Admiral Nimitz -- When he and his original staff were relieved of duty at Berkeley and assgined to other stations, we gave a bon voyage party for them at the then famous Tate's

Restaurant at Gerry and Mason Streets in San Francisco. Although it was prohibition time, we managed to import some very fine wines from our favorite winery in Napa Valley.

In his farewell address, Captain Nimitz complimented and thanked everyone. Then he added some very temperate observations regarding the sometimes un-officer-like conduct of a few of us on our summer cruises. That message came through loud and clear to us culprits.

Q: Excuse me, do you remember his words?

Archer: No, they were not too explicit. But I was serving as master of cerremonies and seated next to him as he was talking, and he laid a gentle hand on my shoulder and gave me a little tap and I got the point that I was one of those to whom he was alluding.

What had happened was that when we had arrived in Victoria or Vancouver; two or three of the people that I have heretofor alluded to had taken a suite of rooms in the old Empress Hotel in Vancouver. We didn't pay too much attention to what we were supposed to be doing while in port. Although he was not on the cruises, the word obviously reached him very soon after we all returned to Berkeley.

Q: I'd like to ask on that point – did you have the feeling that he knew everything that was going on with everybody?

Archer - 11

Archer: I am sure He had a full report on the hours that we were ashore, and the hours that we returned to the ship.

Q: Also, I mean when you were at Berkeley, did you have the feeling -- what was your feeling as to the amount of information he had of the courses and the professors and the students?

Archer: He kept himself very fully informed, I'm sure. For example - When we'd come back from the rifle range, we'd hardly get back to his headquarters and he'd know what our scores were. I know that he knew our grades the day after the various professors filed them.

Q: Did you have the feeling of him being a man of destiny, to use a cliche, that long ago?

Archer: I had a feeling that he certainly was a very outstanding naval officer, a very dedicated naval officer, and a very competent one, very learned. I would have expected that he would certainly have made flag rank. Of course, we did not then anticipate World War II; and five star ranks.

Q: You say very learned, can you give me a for instance?

Archer: I'm sure he was a very prodigious leader. He personally gave some of the lectures on naval warfare and things of that nature.

Then at the very end of his so-called farewell address; he said that he hoped that we would never be called to serve in time of war, but if we were he would be very disappointed if we didn't respond. In his opinion, we had had a very fine training up to that point; and that he would expect us to serve. I, of course, never forgot that admonition.

Q: Where were you in your course, when he left?

Archer: At the end of our junior year, third year. He had us 1926, '27, and '28.

Q: Through the spring of '29.

Archer: That's right. After June of '29, he was relieved. Captain Bruce Canaga succeeded him in the fall of '29, who was I think a classmate of the Admiral's, or one year before or after. They were life-long friends. Captain Canaga served with the Admiral in the Pacific during the war

Then my commission lapsed in 1939 due to inactivity. I went from Berkeley into Law School at Hastings in San Francisco. Then, due to the depressions, I had to drop out of

Hastings and go to a night Law School. I was working my way through Law School, and couldn't engage in any other extra curricula activities; so my commission was revoked in 1939.

When Pearl Harbor occured, I desired to be reinstated immediately. I was restrained for quite a period of time by my family, and by members of my new law firm here in San Diego. I had moved down from San Francisco in September of '41, and just started with this law firm here when Pearl Harbor was hit.

Finally, in April of 1943 I had endured the torment of Admiral Nimitz's admonition that we should serve, if needed. On April 22, 1943; I wrote him an air mail letter. He then was Commander-in-Chief of the Pacific Fleet, of course. I told him that at long last I'd been able to convince my wife and my family and my business associates; that I would seek re-instatement in the naval reserves. My application was in and I had passed a physical examination. I then stated facetiously, this has some significance to what will be related later, "although I fully appreciate that this information will not cause you to change any of your overall strategy for Pacific operations, I thought you might to interested to hear that one more of your original class at California has climbed out of his swivel chair and will endeavor to do something worth while."

Archer - 14

The reason that that has some humorous import is that although Admiral Nimitz was amused and sympathetic to those facetious remarks, and wrote a very nice reply; I later learned - several years later - that Admiral Forrest P. Sherman, his Chief of Staff, thought it was rather impertinent.

After I had had dinner at Admiral Nimitz's table several times at Guam, when we were walking after dinner as we always did, I commented that I thought Admiral Sherman was rather aloof and cold towards me. Then Admiral Nimitz explained to me that it went clear back to my silly letter of April 1943.

Q: That's awfully hard to think that a man would hold that attitude.

Archer: That a young upstart would be writing to his Admiral, and saying that I'm going to come out and try ---

Q: Help win the war.

Archer: Help speed things up.

Q: I wanted to know - what was his reply?

Archer - 15

Archer: Nimitz wrote four days later - "It was a great pleasure to have your letter, and to hear that you're about to rejoin the naval reserve. I hope that you'll have no difficulty securing sea duty in the Pacific. Many of your classmates are in the Pacific Ocean areas. Charles Ide is at present in command of a ship in the Hawaiian area. (He made Captain.) [Ide later] During my visits to the various islands in the Pacific, I've encountered many former California naval ROTC students. It is always a please to meet these men, and I look forward to seeing you hear in the near future. With best wishes, sincerely yours, C. W. Nimitz."

Q: The Institute would be happy to preserve that for you, if you'd like to have them, or at least to have a copy of it.

Archer: I will send you copies of the letter I have aeluded to. I had a very difficult cutting through all the red tape, [to get recommissioned] In spite of the fact that I had a commission as an Ensign and a fully complete file, I had to start all over through the procurement officer at San Diego as if I'd never been anywhere. I have a very voluminous file that I reviewed yesterday and this morning. It's about two inches thick of correspondence with people getting reinstated.

Q: Do you mean that you had to go through complete procurement procedures?

Archer: Yes. Even though, Captain Canaga was then in the Bureau of Personnel in Washington, and I had letters of recommendation from Admiral Nimitz and Admiral Gunther and Captain Canaga and numerous other gentlemen of stature; it just went on and on and on.

Q: How long did it take you to get on active duty?

Archer: August of 1943. I commenced in early April and I finally was recommissioned in August.

I was sent to the Naval Net Depot at Tiberon in San Francisco Bay, where I was under the command of a Captain friend of mine who was giving me a crash refreshment course so that I could get on a combat vessel if possible. While at Tiberon, in the fall of '43, I found the heavy cruiser, LOUISVILLE, CA-28 in Mare Island under going overhaul. We called upon the Captain and asked if I could get duty aboard. He thought it would be fine. Then again I ran into this interminable red tape of getting orders from Tiberon to the LOUISVILLE.

On 12 November 1943, I again appealed to my friend Admiral Nimitz. I told him, "As I first informed you, I was and am extremely anxious to get sea duty aboard a combatant ship in the Pacific. I requested duty here (that was at Tiberon) to get much needed refreshing under the personal supervision of Captain S. M. Haight, my Commanding Officer. That I have had. Recently I began looking around for duty on a ship. The LOUISVILLE I find is presently short of approximately 30 officers. On a visit to the ship I met and conferred with the Commanding Officer, Captain A. S. Wotherspoon who suggested that I make a formal request for duty on his ship; which I have done. My request meets with Captain Wotherspoon's approval. If you have the time, and feel that it is in order, I would deeply appreciate any assistance you can give me in getting orders to the LOUISVILLE. Kindest personal regards, Cordially yours, "

Then, things began to happen rather abruptly. That letter was dated 12 November, and on 17 November '43 Admiral Nimitz directed a letter to Rear Admiral L. E. Denfeld, Bureau of Naval Personnel. I believe at the time he was Chief of Personnel.

"Dear Denfeld, I enclose herewith a letter from one of the graduates from the first Naval ROTC unit to leave the University of California at Berkeley with Naval Reserve commission. You will note that he is now ready for sea duty. I hope you can get him in on the LOUISVILLE. Hope that all goes well with you; and that you and Jacobs and Miss Hess are maintaining your good health and good humor. Personal regards to you all. Sincerely yours, C. W. Nimitz."

Then there was a postscript to me, "Dear Archer, Above has gone into the Navy Department and I hope that it will secure the duty you desire. I'll look forward to seeing you when the LOUISVILLE comes out. Kindest regards and best wishes. Sincerely yours, C. W. Nimitz."

Q: That's a letter to treasure, both of them from him, I think.

Archer: Yes, they are. That's why I have them.

I immediately received orders to the LOUISVILLE. In one final farewell duck hunt up at my brother-in-law's ranch at Courtland, California, not far from Mare Island, I got two boxes of very fine duck which I put in a freezer on the LOUISVILLE. Although the LOUISVILLE did not get into Pearl Harbor on that trip, the ducks got to the Admiral. Thereafter, my brother-in-law continued to send him boxes of ducks through out the rest of the war. The Admiral enjoyed them very much, and I'm sure his mess enjoyed very much.

From time to time the LOUISVILLE would pull in to Guam. On each occasion, at least three of them that I definitely recall, he would send a message to me. He would send his boat out to pick me up to bring me ashore for dinner.

Q: He - Admiral Nimitz?

Archer: Yes. It was during one of our walks after dinner that he told me that he and Mrs. Nimitz had laid awake nights debating on whether or not several of us should have been bilged. And, again without being too specific, made it very clear to me that I was one of the subjects of the discussion.

Finally the Japanese capitulated, the LOUISVILLE had been struck by it's third kamikazi off Okinawa and been back to Pearl for repairs. We were on our way back to the far Pacific to get ready for the invasion of Japan, and had stopped at Guam. That was right at the time that the Japanese capitulated and tendered their surrender.

The Captain of the LOUISVILLE came back to the ship one afternoon and said, "I have called on your friend up on the hill. He has agreed that you should go home immediately." The reason for that was that my first wife was ill and my two little daughters, both of whom are now mothers, were sort of being bounced around from one school to another. Admiral Nimitz knew of that. So, orders were issued for me immediately to leave the LOUISVILLE.

Q: Had he thought of this himself?

Archer: He did. The Captain came back to the ship and said, "Your friend up on the hill has decided that you should go home."

Q: I'm sure that that was a very touching experience for you.

Archer - 20

Archer: It was. I left the ship immediately. I carried only such gear as I could fit into a legal size briefcase, which had some significance later. I went ashore on Guam. I found that the yeoman on the LOUISVILLE had discabobolated the orders, and I was assigned to duty on Guam.

I was intercepted by a very salty Commodore, a rank that had been very seldom used for many years in the Navy. It was a rank between Captain and Rear Admiral.

Q: I think they only did use it during the wartime.

Archer: That's my recollection.

The Commodore informed me that he had studied my jacket or file, and found that I was the only available officer in the area that would qualify as a First Lieutenant and a Gunnery Officer. Therefore, I was going to be assigned to the destroyer BUCK which was leaving immediately for Tokyo. I also had learned just as I was leaving the LOUISVILLE, the LOUISVILLE was being sent on a very special mission to Vladivostok

I immediately hitched a ride up the hill to Admiral Nimitz's headquarters. I arrived drenched and muddy, very unsightly, and extremely unhappy; and completely taken aback by this new turn of events.

As I sat in Admiral Nimitz's waiting room, dripping mud and water on his beautiful navy blue carpet, to the disgust of his flag secretary or Lieutenant; out filed from his private office five Admirals. I cannot recall now who they all were, I didn't recognize all of them. But I did recognize of course Admiral Halsey, Spruance, and Mitscher. The other two I did not recognize or I do not recall. Each was carrying an autographed photograph of the Admiral, and as each one would go through the door the Admiral would slap him on the back and say, "Well done" and call them by name.

Q: You probably never saw that much brass all together in one time before or since.

Archer: No, I'm sure I never did. I don't know how they all got there at the same time.

Q: Yes, it is a question. This was after the war though?

Archer: This was August 26th. After the Japanese, had tendered their surrender.

It later developed in my conversation with Admiral Nimitz that afternoon, that General MacArthur was flying from Baatan to Guam to pick up Admiral Nimitz in the wee small hours of the next morning and they were off to Tokyo. That may be the reason why all these Admirals were assembled there. They, too, probably were going to fly with General MacArthur and Admiral Nimitz or --

Q: At least they all were in Tokyo at the time of the surrender.

Archer: They were there, and they may have been assembled there to go to Tokyo.

Q: Did you say MacArthur was coming from Baatan?

Archer: From Manila on his plane which was called the BAATAN.

Q: Then he picked up Admiral Nimitz and took him on his plane?

Archer: That's right.

Q: That's interesting, I hadn't known that before.

Archer: I was finally ushered into the Admiral's private office. He, of course, was rather exuberant over the fact that it was all over because he had predicted previously that it would be late '47 or mid '48 before we would even attempt to invade Japan.

Q: I think that's a historic moment in his life. If you

hadn't thought of doing it; I wish you would describe what he said, how he looked, and all of these personal things that were certainly a moment of triumph for him.

Archer: It certainly was. He was, as I think I said, exhuberant almost; and in a very jocular mood. He was wearing khaki bermuda shorts and typical Marine Boon-Doc boots. Occasionally, he'd lean back in his chair, and put one of the boots up on his desk; which was not exactly like the Admiral.

Q: No, it seems out of character.

Archer: One of his first remarks to me was, (you asked me earlier about how close track he kept of things that were happening - this is a classic example) I had been advised less than an hour before by this Commodore down on the docks at Guam that I was going to be sent to Tokyo on the BUCK. After very brief greetings, the Admiral said, "I hear you're going to Tokyo on the destroyer BUCK."

Q: How could he have know that?

Archer: I've cogitated about that many many times, and do not know the answer. I forgot to ask him how he ever got that message so quickly. But somehow, he knew about it.

Archer - 24

I said, "No Admiral, I'm not going to go to Tokyo on the BUCK if I can help it at least sir." He just laughed, and he said, "I recall a letter that you wrote to me. Something about you were going to crawl out of your swivel chair and you were going to come out here and help speed this up." (Which wasn't the exact language I used).

Q: But he remembered some of the words.

Archer: He remembered the gist of the letter of April 1943.

Q: That's remarkable.

Archer: And he said, "I know you're a sea lawyer. I think we made a contract. I think you did some share in speeding this up, so you can go on home now." He called the flag Lieutenant in, and asked him to issue me orders sending me to the nearest naval district to my home; which would be the 11stth Naval District in San Diego.

As I mentioned to you before, I was carrying only a legal briefcase; like the one sitting here beside me. I went to the airport on Guam --

Q: Before we leave that, I would to have you describe if you can, his facial expressions.

Archer: He was full of smiles, very very happy that it was over. I questioned him as to whether there might be any trick or trap in this surrender; as our Captain on the LOUISVILLE suggested when we received midway between Pearl Harbor and Guam, the word that the Japs had offered to surrender. Our Captain took a very dim view of it. He thought it was some sort of a trick or trap. I asked the Admiral about that. He said, no he was certain that they were sincere and going to go through with the surrender.

Q: What did his eyes look like?

Archer: They were always kind of sparkly and crinkly. He was obviously very happy.

Q: Was he walking back and forth, moving around?

Archer: No, he was just sitting back, as I said, in a big chair by this big desk or table with one foot cocked up on it.

Q: What time of day was it?

Archer: This was mid-afternoon.

Q: What was the weather like? You spoke of dripping.

Archer: If you've ever been out in that general area, it rains sometime or other every day. I had been caught in a ~~this~~ cloud burst. Then it clears up momentarily. It was a nice day, I just got hit by a quick cloud burst.

Q: It's such a historic moment, and so few people would have seen him on that day; that I was trying to draw you out with every possible small detail you could think of, to make a picture of him at this moment.

Archer: I'll give you one other, I think very historic point.

My father had served under General Arthur MacArthur in the Phillippines in the Spanish-American War. About the time my father was leaving the Philippines, General Douglas MacArthur arrived out there as a Second Lieutenant right out of West Point.

In World War I, my father was Chief of Staff of the division that was in the front lines next to General Douglas MacArthur's division. My father was very awed and respectful of Douglas MacArthur, and resentful of all the criticism that was leveled at him. I carried some of that into the Navy and out into the Pacific.

I'd have arguments in the wardroom with some of my fellow officers about General Douglas MacArthur and his tremendous academic record at West Point and all his decorations for heroism and other accomplishments.

I asked Admiral Nimitz that afternoon, when he told me that General MacArthur was coming to get him in the General's plane and they were going together to Tokyo the next morning, what their relations had been.

As I recall, Admiral Nimitz had complete command of all forces - Navy, Marine, Army - out to a certain parallel. And MacArthur had command beyond that. I don't recall just where the point was.

Q: It was easy to see on the map that MacArthur was in the southwest.

Archer: Admiral Nimitz told me that he had never had any friction or disagreement with General MacArthur whatsoever, at any time, or on any point.

Then, I mentioned how fond my father was of General MacArthur. Admiral Nimitz said, "Will you carry our briefcases to Tokyo?" At that point I made one of the greatest mistakes that I've made in my life. I've made quite a few, but I think that was one of the greatest. I declined.

Q: Oh yes.

Archer - 28

Archer: I did not have the points to get out. I would have made Lieutenant Commander in about two more weeks, I think. But I just thought I might get lost in the shuffle in Tokyo, and be there two or three more years, or come home via the trans-Siberian railroad. So, I declined.

I now, and ever since have very strongly regretted it because another year or six months maybe wouldn't have made much difference with my family life or my legal career.

Q: That was a wonderful offer.

Archer: Oh, tremendous. I told him years later, "Why didn't you issue an order instead of letting me get away?"

Q: That, I think, it typical of him however. But awfully indicative of his character. He gave you this marvelous offer and left it up to you.

Archer: And I goofed.

Q: It may be only in retrospect that you feel that way.

Archer: Anyway, I got this little one sentence order which I never quite understood what it meant. But it certainly got me home. I took it and my brief case out to the airfield at Guam. Although this reads three air priority with an order from Admiral Nimitz, the Commanding Officer at Guam sending me away; I presented this and stood there with my brief case. I left Guam that same night, arrived in Pearl Harbor early the next morning, stood in a line for a very short time, presented the order, and got air priority to San Francisco.

Q: Does Admiral Nimitz's name appear on that?

Archer: Just as Cinc-Pac.

Q: Did he send you here for separation?

Archer: I don't know, I can't make out the order. I got home and I got separated here in San Diego in October. I was assigned no duty here. Upon arrival here, I was just released on my own recognizance; so to speak. Finally, In October I was released from duty.

Q: This doesn't say anything about what the duty was going to be, or why you were coming back, or what you were going to do; does it? Did you never get any other orders?

Archer: No, and I think that's why everybody was so confused; and why I got home so fast. They thought I had part of the treaty in my brief case. They all asked, "Where's your baggage?"

Archer - 30

I said, "I don't have any. I'm traveling light."

Q: This simply gives you traveling authority. It doesn't say anything about your duty or separation.

Archer: I checked in at Pearl Harbor to ComCruPac - I was under this, being on a cruiser - and presented this to a young Commander who was in the first Naval ROTC class at Yale. He said, "You're just the man I'm looking for. You can take this desk and I'm going to go home." I just kept rattling the set of orders. He said, "I can't understand it, but I guess you get to go."

I went out of Pearl Harbor that afternoon. I arrived there about 7 in the morning.

Q: It says for further assignment.

Archer: I never received any further orders or duty.

Q: That's probably the most unusual set of orders anyone ever had.

Archer: I never received too many.

Then, my next contact with the Admiral was when he came to San Diego, I believe it was in 1948, to visit his son who was a naval officer stationed at Coronado. In the meantime, in one of our conversations, the Admiral had told me that he and Mrs. Nimitz had bought a building site on a hill in Marin County overlooking the Bay and the Golden Gate. They planned to build there when he retired. In the meantime, she had decided that it was too cold over there and windy and foggy, she had expressed some concern about whether she wanted to live in Marin County.

I had suggested to him, why not live on Point Loma in San Diego with a mild climate and a beautiful view of the Bay. You could see the ships going and coming. So, when I learned that he was here, I conceived a plan to form a committee of interested individuals, To raise the money and buy them a home on Point Loma.

That idea was not original because my father had done the same thing in San Francisco after World War I. He was the chairman of the committee that raised the money and bought a home for his General, General Leonard Wood, in Pacific Heights in San Francisco.

I thought if father could do that for General Wood, why couldn't I do that for Admiral Nimitz. Somebody told me that his closest personal friend in San Diego was Mauney Pfefferkorn. He is now deceased.

Mauney had been an enlisted man in the Navy when Admiral Nimitz was a junior officer here in San Diego. Pfefferkorn was then a Vice-

President of the First National Bank here in San Diego. I had never met the gentleman. I went over and called on him, and talked to him about this idea.

Within a day or so, Admiral Nimitz came to my office and told me he had heard about it and very sternly admonished me to forget it. That he did not want a gift of a home, from the people of San Diego. I, tongue in cheek, said, "Yes, sir." But I did not erase the idea at all. I planned to go ahead with it. Then in a few more days, he came in, and told me --

Q: I don't like to interrupt you, but when you say, he was stern - again can you describe his face, his manner?

Archer: He just said, "Now look Archer, I don't want you to do this. I don't want you to raise funds to buy Mrs. Nimitz and me a home."

Q: Was he cross?

Archer: Oh, no he wasn't cross, he was just firm.

Q: Was he smiling?

Archer: He was quite bemused by the whole idea that I had even thought of it. I explained where I got the idea. He smiled and said, "Nevertheless, I do not want you to do this."

Q: Did he express appreciation for your idea?

Archer: Yes, he thought it was very nice of me, but just please drop it, forget it.

Q: And then, you said a couple of days later, he came back.

Archer: He said, Governor Knight has invited me to become a Regent of the University of California. Some one's term had expired or was deceased and there was a ten year term, as I recall, open. The Admiral discussed that with me. He thought it would be a very interesting project for him to partake of in retirement. He had developed a very great interest in the University of California; not only due to his three year tour of duty there, but due to all the vast expansion in the atomic energy field in which they were very heavily involved. He thought he would very much enjoy that.

As I have heretofor indicated, he was always very much interested in education - better education. So, he said that he was going to accept that appointment and that of course should necessitate that he live in Berkeley; which he did. He took the appointment, and they bought a home in the Berkeley hills.

Q: Didn't he live at Yerba Buena Island?

Archer: That was after both he and Mrs. Nimitz had injuries. ~~Music come were miceed very beight.~~ They moved out of their home in Berkeley where they had no help and were trying to take care of themselves. The Navy put him in the quarters on Yerba Buena. That was just shortly before he died, a year or so I think. They lived up in the Berkeley Hills for quite a long time after he became a Regent.

While he was on the Board of Regents, I was climbing the ladder to become President of the California Alumni Association. He heard that I was under serious consideration to be a Regent. He wrote me a two-page long-hand letter.

Q: Which I hope you have.

Archer: I'll try to find it. It's not in the files that I brought home yesterday. So, it's got to be in the Regents file or some other personal file. I brought my navy files.

He wrote me this fabulous letter, - "Dear Archer," explaining how arduous the work was as a Regent, how time-consuming. That he didn't believe that I as a young lawyer could serve with complete effectiveness. His classic remark was that, he would be chagrined if one of his shipmates boarded a ship and couldn't be a full member of the crew and was a passenger.

Immediately upon receiving that letter and digesting its full import, I wrote to Governor Knight and told him that while I did not seriously believe he was considering me to be a Regent, if he was, would he please discontinue doing so.

Then my next contacts with the Admiral were in connection with the founding of the University of California here at San Diego. A small group of us conceived this branch of the University. We presented the plan to the Board of Regents, of which Admiral Nimitz was then a member, on December 16th, 1955 at U.C.L.A.

He's not in that picture, unfortunately. The man speaking to the Regents in this picture is John J. Hopkins, Chairman of the Board of General Dynamics. That's my ear that's right behind Mr. Hopkins. I know that the Admiral was down the table there some place, and didn't get in that picture.

Very shortly thereafter, General Dynamics Corporation made a million dollar grant to the University if they would establish this institution for science and mathematics here. We did not then envision a full campus at all. We had in mind a highly scientific establishment comparable to California Tech or M.I.T.

The senior Vice-President of General Dynamics Corporation here on the western coast, Robert Biron, and I took the resolution of a grant of this million dollars to Berkeley. We presented it to President Robert Gordon Sproul, and talked with him about how we could fulfill our ambitions of making a campus here. He suggested two or three key regents that we should call on, among them being Admiral Nimitz. So, Bob Biron and I went immediately out to see Admiral Nimitz. We went up to the Nimitz residence and called on the Admiral and told him of our plans and obtained his very full endoresment.

At that time, he again reminded me of the need of much better instruction in mathametics due to all the technological developments; and reminded me of my shortcomings in that area.

Q: I just think that's incredible that he would remember such details.

Archer: He had a good memory.

He was extremely helpful in our getting this branch of the University here. He was one of the great advocates of it all during the controversial period when they couldn't decide whether to do it or not.

Then in 1960, I became the President of the California Alumni Association. By virtue of the Constitution of the State of California, automatically I became an ex-officio Regent. When I was inducted, Admiral and Mrs. Nimitz were in the front row. He was very pleased. Although he told me not to be one, this was a little different --

Q: You came a different route.

Archer: I would be on the board, and was on the board for two years. If I took an appointment like he had, I would be on either for somebody's unexpired term or the standard sixteen year term. That was what I think he was concerned about - that I'd be devoting the substantial part of my mature life not trying to be a lawyer, but trying to be a decent Regent. That prompted the remark about - please don't be a passenger on this ship.

Then, when I was on the Board of Regents, the move commenced to abolish compulsory ROTC at the University of California. Twice Admiral Nimitz wrote a letter to each Regent. Personal letters addressed to each of the twenty-four regents, urging that they not do that; and suggesting that before they took any action they take the testimony of four members of the first class of Naval ROTC at Berkeley. To whit - Captain Tracy D. Cuttle, Admiral Oonnie P. Lattu, Captain Joseph Chase, and attorney James Archer.

He seemingly forgot that I was then on the Board, when he wrote those letters; or preferred to ignore it. So, that then I was asked by all the Regents - "Why does he want the four of you to testify on the subject?" I facetiously advised my fellow Regents that probably we were the four most incorrigible members of the first class.

Q: And it looked like you had developed.

Archer - 38

Archer: With the exception of myself, the other three-- Lattu was the first Naval ROTC man in the United States to make flag rank; and the other two gentlemen were Captains.

Q: What was the regents action on it? It still is a matter of discussion.

Archer: I'm not sure where it stands now. It's still under debate, back and forth.

Q: I should ask you - you feel that he was a strong supporter of it then?

Archer: Oh, definitely.

Q: You use the word - compulsory, ROTC.

Archer: Yes, under the land-grant system where the Universities throughtout the country obtained land grants from the federal government; they were required to have a course in ROTC. When I entered Berkeley --

Q: The people weren't required to take it, only if they wanted to.

Archer: Oh, no, they were required to take it. Every undergraduate that entered Berkeley in 1926 was required to sign up for ROTC. You were only required to take two years in the Army, and then one could drop out. Many men didn't.

Q: In the Army?

Archer: In the Army. Under Nimitz's program - the Navy's program - they couldn't compel you to say that, "I will take four years"; but you did make a commitment. It wasn't legal or legislatively compulsory on you, but you did make a commitment to him that you would take four years.

Q: He was the first NROTC, but they had had ROTC all the years?

Archer: Army ROTC had been there for years.

The last personal meeting that I had with Admiral Nimitz was on April 5, 1963. They were invited to come here on their 50th wedding anniversary by Mr. James S. Copley, the publisher of the San Diego Union and the San Diego Evening Tribune.

That was arranged by Captain E. Robert Anderson, who was a life-long personal friend of the Nimitz's. And who I understand you are going to interview when he comes back from a trip.

Q: That's correct.

Archer: He can give you much more intimate material than I've been able to give you.

Q: I think this is just wonderful. This is a completely different viewpoint.

Archer: Well, yes.

Q: They did come?

Archer: They came. Captain Anderson, and Mrs. Archer and met them at the airport. I was designated to escort Admiral Nimitz out to LaJolla to called on Mr. Copley. I have a picture here of the three of us at Mr. Copley's desk.

After chatting with Mr. Copley for awhile, I took him up to the new campus which was the first time that he had ever seen the one that he had so strongly assisted in founding.

Q: He was 82 here I believe.

Archer: I do not have that in mind, I'm sorry.

Q: He died in 1966.

Archer: This was April 5, 1963.

Q: He was born in 1885. He would have been 78 years old.

Archer: The Navy car that picked the Admiral and me up at the airport flew a five-star flag, which was the first and only time that a five-star flag has ever flown in San Diego. As you can well imagine, as it drove along the Pacific Highway and through LaJolla a lot of people who were service-connected had their necks turned. He was wearing a cream-white ten-gallon hat that some Texans had given him, which confused the people that were watching us. He was very thrilled at seeing the new LaJolla campus of the University.

Q: What was he wearing - a business suit?

Archer: A business suit.

Q: Is this the picture, is this the same day?

Archer: The same day. Blue suit and vest and stripped tie.
There was a Navy League luncheon at the U. S. Grant Hotel that day. I don't recall who was the guest speaker - you can get this from Captain Anderson. Some high-ranking Naval Officer was here to be the guest speaker.

When this car with the five-star flag came up Broadway and drove around the hotel to the front of it, over the main entrance was a hugh five-star flag. There was quite a buzz with all these navy enlisted men, officers, and people familiar with the navy going to this luncheon. To see a five-star flag drive up was quite something.

I neglected to mention that after we left Mr. Copley's office in downtown LaJolla, we were on our way up here to the campus. I said, "Admiral we will just about pass in front of the home of Admiral Turner Joy's widow. Would you like to stop and give her your regards?" He thought that was fine. She lives just one block from our home here.

We drove in the driveway. In the neighborhood are quite a few retired Army, Navy, and Marine officers and their families. There was quite an outpouring. Very unfortunately - Martha Joy wasn't home.

Q: Isn't that a shame?

Archer: All we could do was leave his card. Neighbors saw who his escort was, and so we received quite a few telephone calls that evening - "What were we doing?"

Q: I'm sure she regretted not being home.

Archer: She did.

Archer - 43.

After the Navy League luncheon, Admiral and Mrs. Nimitz were driven to Orego Hot Springs to Mr. Copley's home there; where they spent about a week thoroughly enjoying swimming.

That was the last time that I saw the Admiral alive.

Q: You speak of swimming. He still was athletic at the age of 78?

Archer: Oh, yes. Both of them were swimming. It was warm and comfortable.

I neglected one thing to tell you. After I saw him giving all of the Admirals the autographed photographs, I had the presence of mind for some strange reason to ask him if I might have one too. Which he agreed to give me.

Months later I received this in the mail, dated 23 October 1945 -- "To James W. Archer, an old friend and shipmate, who did his share in defeating Japan, best wishes, C. W. Nimitz." He couldn't say anything nicer.

Q: No, beautiful. You have made me feel that there was a warmth about Admiral Nimitz that many people who served with him have not given me because they think of him really as the military person or as the good shipmate without giving me the feeling of the personal warmth and characteristics that

Archer - 44

your experiences with him would indicate.

Archer: We had a very warm relationship. I don't know just how it developed, it was there, it was always there as you can tell from '26 to '63.

Q: Do you know anything as to his family relationships? Did he ever speak to you about his family?

Archer: Oh, yes

INDEX

for an interview

with

JAMES ARCHER

Anderson, CAPT E. Robert, 39-41

Archer, Mrs. James, 40

Baatan, 22

Berkeley, 1-12, 33-41

Biron, Robert, 35-36

Buck, 20, 23

California, University of, 1-12, 33-41

Canaga, CAPT Bruce, 12, 16

Chase, CAPT Joseph, 5, 37-38

Copley, James S., 39-40, 42-43

Cuttle, CAPT Tracy D., 3, 5, 37-38

Denfeld, RADM L. E., 17

Depression of 1929, 9, 12

Guam, 14, 18-21, 24-25, 29

Gunther, CDR Ernest L., 3, 6, 16

Haight, CAPT S. M., 17

Halsey, Admiral William Frederick, 21

Hastings Law School, 12-13

Hess, Miss Helen, 17

Hopkins, John J., 35

Ide, Charles, 15

Jacobs, Admiral Randall, 17

Japanese; surrender of, 19, 21-26

Joy, Mrs. Turner (Martha), 42

Knight, Governor Goodwin, 33, 35

Lattu, Admiral Onnie P., 37-38

Louisville, 16-20, 25

MacArthur, General Arthur, 26

MacArthur, General Douglas, 21-22, 26-27

Mitscher, Admiral Marc Andrew, 21

Murphy, Vincent R., 6

Nimitz, Mrs. Chester W., 18, 31-32, 34, 36, 43

NROTC, 1-12, 37-39

Okinawa, 19

Pearl Harbor, 13, 19, 25, 29-30

Pfefferkorn, Mauney, 31

Regents, Board of (University of California) 33-37

Sherman, ADM Forrest P., 14

Sproul, Robert Gordon, 35

Spruance, Admiral Raymond Ames, 21

Tokyo, 20-21, 23-24, 27

West Point, 27

Wood, General Leonard, 31

World War II, 13-30

Wotherspoon, CAPT A. S., 17

Yerba Buena, 34

DECLARATION OF TRUST

The undersigned does hereby appoint and designate as his (her) Trustee herein, the Secretary-Treasurer and Publisher of the United States Naval Institute to perform and discharge the following duties, powers, and privileges in connection with the possession and use of a certain taped interview between the undersigned and the Oral History Department of the United States Naval Institute.

(1) As an <u>Open</u> transcript it may be read (or the tape audited) by qualified researchers upon presentation of proper credentials as determined by the Trustee. In the case of interviews about the late Fleet Admiral C. W. Nimitz, it is intended that first use of the material shall be made by the biographer of the Fleet Admiral, Professor E. B. Potter, and the Naval Institute is authorized to deal with the material in this fashion.

(2) It is expressly understood that in giving this authorization, I am in no way precluded from placing such restrictions as I may desire upon use of the interview at any time during my lifetime, nor does this authorization in any way affect my rights to the copyright of any literary expressions that may be contained in the interview.

Witness my hand and seal this 17th day of February 1970.

Edward V. Beuwd

I hereby accept and consent to the foregoing Declaration of Trust and the powers therein conferred upon me as Trustee:

R. E. Bowke
Secretary-Treasurer and Publisher

Interview with Mr. and Mrs. Edward V. Brewer, Jr.

Place: At their home, 157 Hagar Avenue, Piedmont, California

Subject: Fleet Admiral Chester A. Nimitz

Date: 24 January 1970

By: Etta Belle Kitchen

Q: Commander Brewer is USNR (Retired) and his lovely wife is Marjorie Dean Brewer and she was a naval officer in the Supply Corps, served all during the war, and got out of the Navy at the end of January 1946 as a JG.

It's delightful to be here and I'm awfully glad to have the opportunity to talk with both of you. I'd like to start the tape relating to Admiral Nimitz by asking you how you happen to know him, so either of you can pick this up and go on from there.

Cdr. B.: Well, mine goes back actually to approximately 1927. My father, who was on the faculty at Berkeley, had a home directly across the street from the one that the Admiral, who then was, of course, a commander, rented when he came to Berkeley to found the Navy reserve. So, from that time on, obviously interspersed with his being back in Washington and at sea, I've known the Admiral.

Q: That covers a long time, doesn't it?

Cdr. B.: Yes, it does. Then, actually the more intimate association, though there were some times during the war which I'll tell you subsequently, was when we owned a home in North Berkeley - this was after the Admiral had retired - and

Mr. and Mrs. Brewer - 2

it happened to be right across the street from his home, and we were there for four years, while both our children were just starting to grow up.

Q: So you saw him when you were growing up and observed him as a grown man, really, and then you saw him again after he retired, so you've seen him at both ends of his career, so to speak.

Cdr. B.: That's right.

Q: Well, I'd love to have you both tell me all the things that you can recall and describe, incidents that you observed.

Cdr. B.: Specifically, you mean back in service, active duty time, or subsequently, or...?

Q: Well, keep it in mind that the biographer is going to want to make him a real person, and I would like you to start from the beginning. Any recollections you have from him when you were a child?

Cdr. B.: None particularly there, because they involved primarily growing up with his children who I'd known all the way through. I would say that actual points of interest that would show the type of individual he was and the human aspect of the tremendous individual he was, was, for example, in 1943 when I at that time was on a light cruiser, the Birmingham, and just as we were leaving Pearl Harbor to go out and bombard Wake, as it turned out, an MSG came aboard unbeknownst to me, and

Mr. and Mrs. Brewer - 3

subsequently was handed to me wishing me happy birthday, signed Admiral Nimitz. Now, at that time I was a lowly JG, and for him to take the time, regardless of what kind of a tickler file he had, to do such was quite something.

Q: Heavens, isn't that...? I've heard a lot of stories that told his personal interest in people, but that one is unique, I'm sure.

Cdr. B.: Then were was one subsequently - on that same ship after we'd been torpedoed down in the Solomons after - at Bougainville - we came back to Pearl Harbor and the ship had to be repaired, and at the same time, on the way back, I decided to have an occupational disease called an appendectomy at sea, which necessitated going into Pearl Harbor to the hospital because I had these migraine headaches that sometimes come back from a spinal, you know, and had to lie flat on my back. One day while I was in there, I noticed the nurses scurrying around this room that I occupied with another chap and cleaning everything up, and all of a sudden the Admiral showed up, bringing the San Francisco Chronicle - he thought I might like to see the green sheet, which is the sporting section, and the funnies.

Q: Isn't that absolutely delightful!

Cdr. B.: So this is the type of individual he is. Just fantastic.

Q: Again, it proves the other stories one hears about him, and

Mr. and Mrs. Brewer - 4

all those incidents, I think, are important.

Cdr B.: Right after Tarawa, so he asked me to bring a machine gun captured on Tarawa back to be presented to the University of California, which obviously I acquiesced to do. I came back to port, the ship went up to Mare Island, and with the excitement of getting home, I called, twice got the University and was put off - the President of the University wasn't in town, and with that, forgot about it for about a week or ten days. So, one day I was called up by the skipper of the ship and asked in no uncertain terms, he didn't even know who it was for, of course, where this blankety-blank machine gun was. It seems the Admiral had come in on one of his many secret and quick trips to see his family, his wife, in Berkeley and had seen President Sproul at some party, or something, and asked him how he liked the machine gun, and he hadn't received it. So, I was given a dressing-down to say the least, by our skipper, and then had to commandeer a car and I went down forthwith and delivered the machine gun...

Q: Fortunately it was still there!

Cdr B.: Yes. But in reverse English, the Admiral was not happy with that, to say the least. He was a tremendous human individual, but he was very much of a stickler for regulations,

Mr. and Mrs. Brewer - 5

too.

Q: I think that side of him, of course, had to exist or he couldn't have won the war.

Cdr. B.: Exactly. Now, as far as any other incident - I can't think of anything right at the moment. I think my wife might have some from when we lived there across the street from them at Santa Barbara Road.

Q: Can you remember incidents after he retired? What was your contact with him then?

Cdr. B.: Quite - well - obviously, since we had known him all that time at Santa Barbara Road too when the family was growing up, we'd become well acquainted with them, so, while we were living in Southern California subsequently for 12 years, every Christmas when we came up to see my family, it was always a point of protocol, so to speak, and very happily so, to call on the Admiral and Mrs. Nimitz, which we did every year with the children. So we have known him all the way through from that time on - from the time of the end of the war, I should say, and after he'd retired in Berkeley, we knew him quite intimately, used to be at his home a lot. We'd watch the Victory at Sea television programs, with the children growing up taking little trips with him, like down to Santa Clara Fair because, as you know, he was quite a horse shoe enthusiast...

Q: Tell me about that.

Cdr. B.: I used to play horse shoes with him quite a lot. He

Mr. and Mrs. Brewer - 6

had a horse shoe pit in his - back of his house on the Santa Barbara Road there, and I used to play with him every weekend and sometimes, even, during the week.

Q: Was he good?

Cdr. B.: He was excellent, very excellent. But occasionally I could beat him.

Q: Oh, good! I knew that he was a horse shoe pitcher enthusiast, if that's the way you...

Cdr. B.: Well, he was that, as it's been written up many times. He had a pit, I believe, out at his quarters in Ewa, just outside Pearl Harbor, and used to pitch during the war years.

Q: Right. Tell me what he was like in his home.

Cdr. B.: A most gracious host, as you undoubtedly have heard, a very pleasant person. He was full of witticisms. Unfortunately, my memory doesn't serve me well as to what those all were, but he was just a delightful, relaxed individual. Totally devoid of any of the aspects of military bearing, so to speak, except by obvious perfect carriage. Up to just near the end of his life, why, he still stood just as erect as ever...

Q: How would he greet you at the door?

Cdr. B.: Unfortunately, he was one of the few people - I say unfortunately because he's the only man I ever respected that called me "Eddie." I hate that word, but that's the way he always greeted me.

Q: Well, tell me one word...

Mrs. B.: His greeting, as you came in the door, was, " come on in, come on in. Is there something I can do for you or... Come on in and sit down."

Q: Did he answer the door himself?

Cdr. B.: Oh, yes.

Q: And how would he greet you? Would he put his arm around you? Would he kiss you?

Mrs. B.: Yes, very often. "Midge, it's so good to see you," and a kiss and just as though it may have been a year since you'd seen him.

Q: Would he put his arms around you?

Mrs. B.: Yeah, or on your shoulder, and greet the children. Of course, they thought of the Admiral and Mrs. Nimitz as a third set of grandparents. This was the feeling. I mean, it was the warmth that came from the man to the children, which children sense.

Q: Oh, sure! And, Mr. Brewer, how did he greet you, besides calling you "Eddie"? Did he put his arm around you, shake your hand? Picture yourself as a biographer trying to write of an incident and tell him the detail that he would like to know.

Cdr. B.: I think basically on the man-to-man basis of a hand-

Mr. and Mrs. Brewer - 8

shake more than the - oh, he might have thrown the arm round, but I believe basically it was a man-to-man relationship of a handshake, but a very warm one.

Q: Was he a toucher? You know, some people like to touch other people.

Cdr. B.: No, no. Definitely not.

Q: Was there always a degree of reserve with him that was...?

Cdr. B.: No - well, I guess you could say there was, although I attributed it, if there was any, to the fact of the - to the length of time that he was in the service. I don't think that a person would actually end up being quite the type of individual, let's say, that you'd meet in the business world, in sales work, in which you get the, you know, the very effervescent individual that's enveloping you. There was just a modicum of reserve there, but just the kind that you would respect in a man of that age...

Q: Really warmth, there was a twinkle in the eye?

Cdr. B.: Oh, yes. I didn't ever think of him as not being an extremely warm individual and warm relationship in discussion, but there was always just a modicum of reserve, which you would want.

Q: Did you ever see him slouch or put his feet on a stool, or this kind of thing?

Cdr. B.: Oh, he used to like to take sun baths. You'd see

him outside, stripped down to his waist, and just kind of lying there taking a sun bath. Yeah, he - as far as his dress, once he was retired, except when he was going out, obviously, to a social call, he was most nonchalantly dressed. He had shorts on and an old pair of GI shoes and probably no skivvy shirt, even.

Mrs. B.: We lived across the street, on the up side of the street. The only time we could look down on the Admiral, because he wasn't a man - you looked down upon, and I could always determine how cool it was outside and what clothing to put on the children, because the Admiral would be out working in his yard, and if it was a cool day, he started out with a heavy wool shirt on and heavy wool shorts and the high knee socks and boots. And, as it got warmer, he'd strip off the heavy shirt and maybe have a T-shirt on, and if it was really hot, he'd get down - the shoes would be off for a loafer sort of thing, the high socks would go, and then - he'd be in simple working shorts and even, sometimes, quite short shorts. You could tell how hot it was by looking over and seeing what he had on.

Q: He was your barometer, huh?

Mrs. B.: Oh, he was marvelous.

Q: Do you know what food he liked to eat? What he liked to drink?

Cdr. B.: Well, that was according to the food. He liked everything, I think, but I don't know that specifically, so I shouldn't answer that, but there was...

Q: Well, you've eaten in his home, I presume?

Cdr. B.: Oh, yes. It was a general type of food. I mean, his wife was an excellent cook, and Mrs. Nimitz prepared, as you know, their own food. She didn't have any help, though they could have. Now, I'm not speaking of when they lived on Goat Island, but rather in North Berkeley when they lived on Santa Barbara Road. He had a very famous drink, as you know, called CinCPac, which was rather lethal and his own concoction, he said, and he gave the recipe to his daughter, Nancy, who lives down in Santa Monica, Topanga Canyon, and that was conceived out in Pearl Harbor during the war, due to the shortage of sugar and due to the fact you had to take so many rations of rum with whisky, you may recall, at least that was the ration out there, apparently.

Q: Oh, you mean when you bought - you had to take so much rum along with the whisky. I see what you mean. You took a rum, then you could get a whisky, sort of thing.

Cdr. B.: Yes. It had some sugar. It's basically supposed to be an old-fashioned, but it was using rum instead of sugar, along with whisky, and it's a very lethal drink. A couple of them and you can start talking to yourself pretty well. He had those all pre-mixed, and in gallon jugs, so all they needed to do was to be iced, and he'd serve those. And we learned rapidly that two was about right.

Q: Was he much of a drinker?

Mr. and Mrs. Brewer - 11

Cdr. B.: To a degree - not overly. I never saw, if you're asking, I never saw him happy, I mean, from the point of view of inebriation. Nothing like that.

Q: Oh, no, I wouldn't expect that. But would he serve as many as you wanted, or would he...

Cdr. B.: Yes, oh, yes.

Q: Never any restriction or thought that the Admiral only drinks one or two?

Cdr. B.: No, ~~oh, no~~.

Mrs. B.: Very often when we lived on Santa Barbara Road, we'd be working on our yard and he'd be working in his, he'd call over, "Come on over and have a beer or a glass of sherry. Sun's over the yard arm, we've worked enough."

Q: Oh, that's cute! Now, I do want to talk a little bit about dates. You spoke of different periods. Can you date those events? When were you, as children, close to him?

Cdr. B.: I myself, as a child?

Q: Yes.

Cdr. B.: Well, I was from 1927 when he - my recollection is that he was there. Of course, I was quite young, as you can appreciate, and so I don't recall this except by hearsay, but I know that he was at the Naval Unit here at Berkeley, I believe, for three years. So it was approximately three years that I was growing up with his children there. Then he left

Mr. and Mrs. Brewer - 12

and went, I think, back to the Bureau of Navigation, and then subsequently to sea, and so forth. So that was actually the last time that I knew them that closely in relationships, except when he'd pop in and maybe have my family and myself out to - when he had BatDiv 1, I think, out to the ship out here in the harbor, or something of that nature. But this other episode I'm referring to is approximately 1949, '50, '51, and '52.

Mrs. B.: We moved in to Santa Barbara Road...

Q: That was when you were living across from him...?

Cdr. B.: On Santa Barbara Road. Yes.

Q: And this is in Berkeley?

Cdr. B.: In Berkeley. Right.

Q: I'm trying to identify dates and places. So they were both Berkeley, and one was about three years from '27 to '30, and the other was...

Mrs. B.: Santa Barbara Road ~~The other one - we moved in...~~

Cdr. B.: About '49 or '50.

Mrs. B.: The spring of '51 until we moved south in January of '54..

Cdr. B.: I can see my wife does better on dates.

Q: Oh, so it was '51 to '54, the second episode? And that was

Mr. and Mrs. Brewer - 13

Santa Barbara Road in Berkeley and...?

Mrs. B.: That's correct. He was at 728 and we were at 727.

Q: I see. And now those were the two times when you actually lived close to...?

Cdr. B.: Right.

Q: Thank you. You spoke of something that I wanted to pursue, saying of secret and quick trips home during the war. Can you expand on that any?

Cdr. B.: All I know is from what he or his wife has said along the line. I can't specifically say when they happened. But it was his custom when he could to fly in to San Francisco quite often. Those were, I'm certain, to meet officials from Washington, but at the same time - his wife was living at that time - south of the campus on Forrest Avenue, and he'd drop in and see her and his one daughter who was still at home. But how often that happened, I don't know. He'd drop in unannounced to his family, as far as I know.

Q: Do you know - I heard a story of his having special coffee - a special brew for coffee. Do you know anything about that?

Cdr. B.: I think again his daughter Nancy could better enumerate that because she has that same secret formula. It's, believe me, really Navy coffee. It's made out of several blends, and extremely strong. If you drink expresso, it's better than espresso, in its strength.

Mrs. B.: They used to get the beans and grind them quite often.

Cdr. B.: Yes. Oh, yes, it's made from ground zero. Nancy does too.

Mrs. B.: The sort of a man he was physically, you used to tell how he'd be out there jogging and all sorts of exercises in the morning - not jogging but doing exercises. He took care of his body...

Cdr. B.: Oh, well, that was typical of the man. What Midge is referring to is back in 1927 when he was living across from my family there in North Berkeley - incidentally, that was Bay View Place, he had rented this home - he'd be out every morning skipping rope and shadow boxing, and though jogging was not the word then, it was the same thing. He was up doing his calisthenics every morning. Extremely active. And then subsequently, when we knew him later in his retirement back there in 1949 to '50, he was very active doing all the work in the garden. THe extensive work, I mean digging and so forth. He kept himself in excellent shape right up to the time he started having health problems.

Q: Now, can you think of any incident that you would know that nobody else would know?

Mrs. B.: I can. There are incidents involving the children and the human side...

Cdr. B.: Other than the ones that I enumerated, those little episodes...

Q: But do you recall the early years, the '27 to...?

Cdr. B.: No. You see I was only about in my early teens, so that would have been hearsay, and I don't actually recall any hearsay ones. My family obviously would, but I...

Q: You don't recall any conversations, or was he ever - you didn't know he was going to be CinCPac in those days!

Cdr. B.: Obviously. No, there are no particular episodes I could recall then. He had his loyalty to his friends in the Navy was tremendous, as we know. A lot of people enumerate this. A very dear friend of his was, I think, a classmate or close to being a classmate - Captain Canega - who subsequently had the Navy Unit at Berkeley, and the Captain had physical reversals later in life, much earlier than the Admiral did, and he spent many times doing things for the Captain...

Q: Financial you mean?

Cdr. B.: I don't know whether it was financial or not. I wouldn't be surprised, but I have no knowledge of that.

Q: This is something you heard of?

Cdr. B.: I know of. I mean...

Q: You know of?

Cdr. B.: I know that he spent a lot of time with the Captain

Mr. and Mrs. Brewer - 16

and his family helping in any way he could.

Q: I think that's interesting. Now, can you expand on that?

Cdr. B.: No, I can't because I just know that little bit about it. I don't know anything more than that.

Q: This would be what period of his life?

Cdr. B.: That was after the war.

Q: But you know that he called on him?

Cdr. B.: Oh, yes. Many times.

Mrs. B.: The Captain would come up and bring plants to the Admiral, and they shared a love of the garden.

Q: And you don't know whether he helped him financially?

Cdr B.: No. I don't know whether that was involved or not.

Q: So may be emotionally and morally, it was?

Cdr. B.: Yes, because...

Mrs. B.: They were close friends.

Q: How do you spell that name?

Cdr B.: C-a-n-a-g-a. Captain Canaga's son is in the Navy, too, and is a doctor, and I think a captain also. Anyway, when we *there is no page 17*

Mr. and Mrs. Brewer - 18

were living down south, for example, and this will lead into me saying some other things about when the childred were young, he came down at one time and we asked if it would be possible that he - if he could drop by and at that time I was very active in the Scouts, as my son was, and to make the story short, he came and had his picture taken with the whole Scout troop and let them talk to him and ask him any questions they wanted to, and giving them all autographed pictures, and, as you know, he was very free with passing out pictures of himself to anybody that ever wanted one, including them, he'd also pass out to the kids, match folders with the Fleet Admiral on it with five stars and...

Q: Now, is that at the same time?

Cdr B.: That time and subsequently, many times, he's done that to our children and other people I know. He's given - was always giving those folders out.

Q: That's cute, isn't it? Well, now can you pinpoint the date that you're speaking about when he came to Santa Monica and spoke to the Boy Scouts?

Mr. and Mrs. Brewer - 19

Cdr. B.: That's - gosh

Mrs. B.: The Scout troop had come up to San Francisco. There were 50 boys from the troop, this wasn't the whole troop, and this was an Easter vacation - it was an Easter, so it was in the spring and they had hoped to see the Admiral when they were up here, but it was the time of their fiftieth wedding anniversary, and they had gone south. The boys had hoped to see him, and we had made arrangements when they got back for them to do so. They then met the Admiral at our house in Santa Monica...

Q: Would you know what year that would be approximately?

Mrs. B.: I could check it.

Q: Well, I meant just within what years?

Mrs. B.: Well, our son was in scouting - and you have to be 12 to go into scouting - and he was probably in his first or second year at scouting, and our son is now 18.

Q: Well, can you subtract from that?

Mrs. B. About five, six - well, I can check their wedding anniversary, that would be easier.

Q: I think it's important to put it in its proper sequence, because a biographer would be oral guessing.

Cdr. B.: Right. It was sometime - well, Midge will look that up while we're talking.

Mr. and Mrs. Brewer - 20

Q: Now, do you know any of his stories? I think you said - I'm going to go on interviewing your wife in just a few minutes because I know she has a lot of interesting things -

Cdr. B.: Unfortunately, my memory doesn't serve me at all as far as stories. I'm afraid I don't have any.

Q: You speak of witticisms - did he have a way of greeting somebody with "You look pretty," or "How do I look," or any phrase analogy that you can recall?

Cdr. B.: No, I don't think there's any particular ones that I can think of.

Mrs. B.: It was always, "It's so good to see you," particularly if you hadn't seen him for a while.

Cdr. B.: Yes, but not any particular...

Mrs. B.: No. A twinkle in his eye, I think...

Q: Do you remember what he said to you when he called on you in the hospital?

Cdr. B.: That's a good question. No, except he said that - I do recall this - he said, other than the general conversation with me, just "how are you," and "how are you coming along, are you being taken care of all right," and, of course, I said yes...

Q: Yes, Sir!

Cdr. B.: Very definitely. He said subsequently that, getting up, "Why don't you drop up to my quarters ~~to night~~ to say goodbye?" So I obviously did. It was just before the ship left, so I went in and obviously very formal. I mean, there was ~~no~~ nothing but a formal thing because I was ~~obviously~~ just a lieutenant then.

Q: This was in his quarters or his office?

Cdr. B.: His office. And I was ushered in to his office and he said, as I was standing at almost attention, though he told me to be at ease, and he said, "I suppose you'd like to know if you'll be home anywhere near Christmas," and I said, "Yes, Sir, it would be very nice." I think we'd been out about a year then, something like that, and so he flicked a switch and said to somebody -- I don't know what rank, but I think it was a captain if I recall correctly - "What's the ETA of the Birmingham to Mare Island?" And it came back that we'd be leaving Pearl Harbor on such and such a day, I don't recall the exact day, but we made it back, I think, in four and a half days at 27 knots, and we'd be arriving in Mare Island on December 24th. So that was just his way of letting me know that everything was going to be fine at home.

Q: Well, that again is a cute experience. See, now these you forget, and no one but you would know that because that happened just to you, and that's why I'm trying to dig in your memory to bring up some more of these things...

Cdr. B.: Right, I appreciate it.

Q: ...that perhaps only you can know.

Mr. and Mrs. Brewer - 22

Mrs. B.: That was the spring of '63.

Q: So the spring of '63 was when he took the occasion to meet with the Scouts.

Mrs. B.: To meet with selected Scouts - the Scouts had to vie for this honor of meeting him.

Q: Now, tell me, again, where it was and what happened.

Mrs. B.: It was at our home in Santa Monica. It was on Easter and he and Mrs. Nimitz came and they stayed on for supper with us and Nancy was with them. He met with the Scouts and they had a photographer there who took some pictures for the Santa Monica Evening Outlook, and the Scouts enjoyed it. And he talked to the Scouts at that time he said he felt that scouting developed one of the finest leaderships in boys, and he said you find many of your leaders, or the majority of them, have had scouting in their background.

Q: Isn't that interesting?

Mrs. B.: He was speaking specifically then of Navy leaders, and how much the Navy respected those who had gone on to be Eagles.

Q: That's interesting, isn't it?

Mrs. B.: Yes.

Q: And a real leadership, good comment, I think.

Mr. and Mrs. Brewer - 23

Mrs. B.: I know they were interested in a troop in North Berkeley. Mrs. Nimitz mentioned they were doing this with the scouting, and there may be a Nimitz award in the Scout troop. I don't know.

Q: That's interesting, and it might be pursued.

Mrs. B.: I don't know whether their son was in that troop or not.

CDR B.: Yes, he was.

Q: Now, I'm just about to transfer to Mrs. Brewer, but, again, to try to dredge up things in your memory, do you have any other incidents.

CDR B.: No, except that I should reiterate one thing. Even though I had those personal contacts during the active duty time with him and those two brief instances - or three - that in no way colored anything that he felt I should have in the Navy. What I'm trying to say by that - he in no way pulled any strings to get me better duty or anything like that. I was just another guy named Joe as far as active duty time was concerned, and while I will admit that some of my superiors on the ship when they learned that I knew him tried to fawn around me a little bit to see if that would help out...

Q: Did they really?

Cdr. B.: It was really pathetic.

Q: I think that's interesting.

Cdr. B.: It didn't do them a bit of good.

Q: I don't know but it would seem that a biographer might find that of some interest. Can you expand on that a little more?

Cdr. B.: Well, nothing except that when an MS$ came on board, for example, signed by the Admiral addressed to a JG, it was needless to say, it went around the ship pretty fast that a lowly JG knew the Admiral, and I noticed a marked difference in a few of the senior officers in their attitude to me, which didn't impress me one bit.

Q: No, but I guess that's human nature.

Cdr. B.: Oh, sure. No, but I want to reiterate, though, that there was no choice duty or anything of that nature, or special dispensations as far as orders were concerned, or leave time or anything of that nature.

Q: No, but I think he has. I know that he did do that for one man whom I did interview, and I think that's perfectly appropriate, really.

Cdr. B.: Well, in a way, except that, not to me, not to my way of thinking. I feel that the strength of the man, the great human qualities he had, coupled with the fact that he was completely regulation. One little incident, for example, will show how that is, and this I wasn't going to mention because it doesn't mean too much, but I might bring this out. I can recall just one thing about this time of visiting aboard when he was Admiral, I think, of Battle Division I, three battleships that came into San Francisco, and when we went out to go aboard, and then I was just a teenager, the only recollection I have of that, coming aboard, was approximately - supposedly 500 yards, but it must have been about 500 feet away from the ship, we were coming aboard with him, and everybody topside had to be at attention when he came aboard - everybody - could be in the foretop or any other part of the ship...

Q: What grade was he then?

Cdr. B.: He was Admiral - a rear admiral, then.

Q: Now, what year was this again?

Cdr. B.: Oh, dear, somewhere back in the thirties. I can't say when.

Q: But he was a rear admiral? And how did you happen to be going out on the ship?

Cdr. B.: Well, only through my father and we were friends of his, and he invited my father, my mother, and myself out to...

Mr. and Mrs. Brewer - 26

Q: To have dinner aboard the ship?

Cdr. B.: To dinner aboard the ship.

Q: I see, and what kind of a conveyance..?

Cdr. B.: Oh, it was the Admiral's barge.

Q: The Admiral's barge, and when he came aboard there was no doubt that...

Cdr. B.: It was complete regulations. There wasn't any nonchalance about it, so - this, of course, is what I feel is the way it should be.

Q: Sure.

Cdr. B.: He was the top man.

Q: Well, the greatness has to go both ways. Apparently he was great in his personal life. But I think you've told some interesting vignettes of the man.

Cdr. B.: I hope it helps out a little bit.

Q: Well, you probably will think of others while we're talking to Midge - may I say Midge?

Mrs. B.: Please do.

Q: I wish you could show your picture on tape - both of you - because you're a beautiful couple, and you happen to be particularly pretty. So I want to turn to you, but not to exclude your husband. Can you start with your first contact with Admiral Nimitz and tell all.

Mrs. B.: I think the first time I ever met the Admiral - although I'd heard of him many years - he was invited to our wedding - he was in Washington at the time we were married in June of '46...

Q: Where?

Mrs. B.: In Montclair, New Jersey. And subsequently the Admiral said, if I'd known you then as I know you now, we would have been there.

Q: Oh, that's a cute comment.

Mrs. B.: But they got many invitations to many weddings, and they knew Ed, but they didn't know me, which I took as quite a compliment when he said it.

Q: Well, it's a cute comment.

Mrs. B.: This is a typical comment of the Admiral's, and, of course, he knew I'd been in the Navy and apparently looked up my record.

Q: Had he?

Mrs. B.: I guess so because he had to know some of these details...

Q: Tell me what makes you say that.

Mrs. B.: Well, this will come in a little later.

Mr. and Mrs. Brewer - 28

Q: But you won't forget!

Mrs. B.: No, I won't. We met him when we were looking for a home...

Q: Now, where were you?

Mrs. B.: We were renting a home in Berkeley at the time, and we were buying a home, and this is when we bought our home on Santa Barbara Road, and we looked at the house...

Q: This would be 19...?

Mrs. B.: '50 - '51, about March.

Q: That was the first time you met him?

Mrs. B.: Yes, and the person that was showing us the home, a realtor who lived right near where Mrs. Nimitz did during the war, Forrest Avenue, so that she knew the Nimitzes and they saw us, saw the house then, and we told them we were considering buying the house, and they tried to discourage us.

Q: What do you mean, they saw you?

Mrs. B.: We were coming out of the house...

Q: And they recognized you?

Mrs. B.: They recognized my husband immediately, and they recognized the realtor who was with us, also.

Q: Were they in their house and saw you?

Mr. and Mrs. Brewer - 29

Mrs. B.: He was in the yard.

Q: Strictly a coincidence?

Mrs. B.: Yes, and so they tried to discourage us from buying the house, not because they didn't want us as neighbors, but the house had 57 steps to the front door, and I was quite pregnant with our son. And we did buy the house, but they were just - oh - so gracious in every way, and I remember one thing they said when we moved in, being quite pregnant and I had a daughter who was then not quite two, and Mrs. Nimitz and the Admiral, both, said, "Now any time you have to go to the hospital, day or night, call on us to take over on your daughter. After all, we took care of her father when his sister was born." This was when my husband lived across the street from the Admiral when the Admiral was ~~down~~ at the Naval Unit here.

Q: So they had taken care of his sister - is his sister older?

Mrs. B.: ~~Yes,~~ No, she ~~was~~ is eight years his junior, and they took care of my husband...

Q: When his sister was born?

Mrs. B.: Yes. We didn't have to call on them for that, although we did call on them for other things. But the children, I know, would sit on the balcony we had and they'd see the Admiral out on the front lawn and they'd yell, "Hi, Admiral." They couldn't say it quite right, but they thought he was just a marvelous person. He always greeted them warmly and has

Mr. and Mrs. Brewer - 30

followed them all the way through, as long as he was alive he followed what they were doing.

Q: You and your husband are the ages of his children - of Admiral Nimitz' children, is that right?

Mrs. B.: Ed and the Admiral's second daughter are 13 days apart in age, and Mrs. Nimitz always said when she punished Nancy she felt that she had to punish Ed, too, because they were in it together.

Q: Well, now, go on with other incidents and times you saw him, and anything you can think of.

Mrs. B.: Well, I can remember in '53 our son was quite ill, and I can pinpoint this to their 40th wedding anniversary. Our son was ill and had to get to the doctor, at his office, and I had to have somebody to hold him as I drove him to the doctor's. So I called over to ask Mrs. Nimitz if she could ride with me, just to hold him, not realizing the Admiral had come back from Washington that day, and the Admiral answered the phone and he said, "Midge, I'll be right over and help you," and I said, "I'll meet you by the car." And so I brought our son down and the Admiral held him. Well, he had a cold, he'd flown from the East to the West - I think he came back for somebody's funeral, one of the five-star admirals' funeral - and he went with me to the doctor. His ears were plugged up, he couldn't hear. We got home. He insisted on carrying our son all the way up to the house, all 57 steps, and, here, it was their wedding anniver=

sary, ~~while I.~~.

Q: How old was your boy then?

Mrs. B.: About a year and a half.

Q: So he was a little fellow.

Mrs. B.: Oh, yes. That's why I couldn't just have him sit in the car - but this is the sort of thing he would do, and, rather than send a plant to them, I baked a cake and decorated it all, had camellias around it, and took it over, and had drawn ~~and~~ the five stars and their initials on it. And he couldn't get over that even with a sick child I would take time to do this. But of course he helped me out, too.

Q: Yes, but I can appreciate how he felt.

Mrs. B.: Yes. Then I remember another incident - they always got such a kick out of watching the children and what they were doing. In another incident, we went over one day, we'd been working in the yard as he had, and at noon, he said, "Sun's over the yardarm, come on over and have a beer or a sherry," and we went over and the children came, and there was a hose going, watering a tree, just a trickle, and our son picked up the hose, stood in front of where you would turn off the faucet, put his finger over the hose, and squirted all of us - Admiral included, everybody.

Q: How old was your boy then?

Mrs. B.: He was about the same age. He was under two. I

have pictures of it.

Q: Precocious!

Mrs. B.: No. There's something fascinating to all men, I think, about a hose, and they just thought this was the funniest thing ever.

Q: The men thought it was funny?

Mrs. B.: Oh, the Admiral just roared. He just thought it was marvelous. It wasn't going that fast, we didn't get that wet, but immediately they had to take pictures.

Q: And you do have some?

Mrs. B.: Yes.

Q: I'd love to have some...

Mrs. B.: The Admiral's not actually in the picture. They always got a cute one of - our daughter, she was two years older, so she would be about four when she used to help her father wash the car, and she looked like the worst moppet, but they just thought that was hilarious watching Pam. We've got pictures of her washing the car - just soaking wet. But they just enjoyed - he would just burst out with a hearty laugh at what the children were doing.

Q: Did he seem to enjoy Mrs. Nimitz?

Mrs. B.: Yes. He was devoted to her.

Q: Did he ever speak of her? Did you ever see him without her? Of course, you did, on occasion. Would he speak of her? How and in what manner?

Mrs. B.: Very affectionately.

Q: What did he call her?

Mrs. B. Catherine.

Q: Always Catherine?

Mrs. B.: Always Catherine. I've never heard him speak of her as anything else, but it was not a harsh "Catherine," it was a soft "Catherine."

Q: An affectionate "Catherine"!

Mrs. B.: Yes. No, they were devoted.

Q: I'm sure you have more. Don't let my interruptions stop you.

Mrs. B.: Well, we used to go over and watch <u>Victory at Sea</u>, and our children would go over, and they would sit there glued to the TV, and the Admiral was always - if we had a drink when we were there, they always had something, and he always had some - something different he wanted them to try...

Q: For the children?

Mrs. B.: For the children. At one time it might be a grapefruit mixture of some sort or - you can tell better the various things that he used to give them - but they looked forward to it - what's the Admiral going to have this time?

Q: That is a cute thing to do, isn't it?

Mrs. B.: Yes. And when we saw them in subsequent years, we used to come up at Christmastime and we'd always have to see the Admiral. It was just like seeing your grandparents - which is what they expected.

Q: And he always had some special thing for them?

Mrs. B.: Something different for them.

Q: I started to ask the kinds of food they had, and then I don't think I let you finish the question - finish the answer.

Mrs. B.: I think their food was always interesting. Mrs. Nimitz saw to that. He did a bit of cooking.

Q: Tell me about that.

Mrs. B.: I've never had anything particularly that he fixed, but I know he would help her in cooking things, when the two of them were alone.

Q: Did he have a special field? Or do you know that?

Mrs. B.: No. I don't. I can't recall any. I don't know whether this has ever been brought out, but he actually had applied for the - I believe he tried out for West Point.

Q: Yes, he did.

Mrs. B.: And instead he got Annapolis. I remember one night when we were there for dinner, it was on the tenth anniversary of Pearl Harbor, he always used to introduce me as a wire rope expert, just because I was in Controlled Materials, and apparently one of the only few WAVES that got into the field, At Harvard when we were in supply school training. I think there was one paragraph on the whole thing, but I ended up in that, I guess through a freak thing. But this is how I have reason to believe that he had checked into my records a bit. He may not have, but there was a little glimmers of things.

Q: He probably did.

Mrs. B.: Probably, and that night he was telling about ten years ago...

Q: Before we get to that. How did he react to seeing <u>Victory at Sea</u> on the TV?

Mrs. B.: I think - he had seen some of it prior to the time it was actually shown on the TV. So that I don't believe - I don't recall his specific reactions. He watched it as we all did.

Q: Did he think it was good, bad, or...?

Mrs. B.: Oh, excellent-

Q: That's what I mean.

Mrs. B.: Yes.

Q: Did he say, "That isn't true," or...?

Mrs. B.: No. I don't ever recall him saying that wasn't true,. Do you, dear?

Cdr. B.: No. As a matter of fact, I have a pretty good suspicion that he was consulted pretty strongly about it...

Mrs. B.: At least the Navy phase of it.

Cdr. B.: ...to the extent that he had seen this, as Midge said, I think he had seen these pictures before they were put on commercially on the TV.

Q: Yes, I would imagine so, because the Navy...

Cdr. B.: Therefore, his reaction was not like mine when I saw it...

Q: It wasn't an original...?

Cdr. B.: No. When I saw my ship blown up and I was on it, why, that brought me right out of my chair, but it didn't phase him particularly.

Mrs. B.: I remember your comment to him at the time was, "who the heck was around taking pictures?"

Q: That's always a question in one's mind. Did he answer you when you said that, or just...?

Cdr. B.: No. No, to the best of my recollection.

Mrs. B.: I think it was made as a statement or an exclamation

Mr. and Mrs. Brewer - 37

point, rather than a question.

Q: You said - and I want to explore this - that when he retired he only brought one person with him. Can you expand on that a little bit?

Cdr. B.: Well, just to this extent. I'm told by comparison, as you probably know, that General MacArthur, who had the same equivalent rank, had a retinue of officers and enlisted personnel at his beck and call. The Admiral was entitled - and this I only know by hearsay, as to the exact nomenclature of the personnel, but I believe that he was entitled to several officers, including a captain, commanders, and lesser officers, and enlisted personnel, but he felt that for his simple needs as he - for any official duties, why, he had one sergeant in the Marine Corps, and that was it.

Q: Was that Mr. Cozard?

Mrs. B.: Yes.

Cdr. B.: Now, Cozard could tell you more about it, actually. He could tell you what the other personnel were. But he did not, except when there were official duties and then there would be officers assigned to him while he...

Q: You spoke of Mrs. Nimitz doing the cooking. Did they have any help at all?

Mrs. B.: They had a cleaning girl occasionally, and if they had a large party, they would have domestics that they would hire.

Mr. and Mrs. Brewer - 38

Q: When they lived on Goat Island, they...

Cdr. B.: Oh, there they had all - yes, they were all Filipinos, the boys that they had.

Mrs. B.: Of course, part of the reason was that living on a naval base - you see, that was an official residence, and they took care of the maintenance.

Cdr. B.: Plus the fact Mrs. Nimitz was becoming more incapicitated then, too.

Q: Why did they move - or do you know the circumstances of their moving...?

Cdr. B.: Basically because of her.

Mrs. B.: And his health.

Cdr. B.: Well, his health was failing a bit, but her - as you know, she has to walk with canes and is extremely crippled, and she just couldn't...

Mrs. B.: She couldn't handle the stairs there at home. It was a two-story home, and also at one time the Admiral was sick and he fell, and she was downstairs, and she couldn't get him into bed, and they didn't want to have to have somebody live in. I don't know who arranged it, but it was arranged. Suddenly this quarters became available and...

Cdr. B.: Well, the Navy amalgamated the two commands, and then this one official residence was available.

Mr. and Mrs. Brewer - 39

Q: I see. Do you know more about his falling, or...?

Mrs. B.: No, I think he slipped. He'd had a fever. I don't know any more than that. They took him, after he fell, out to the hospital and then it was while he was there getting over this 'flu bug or pneumonia or whatever it was, that suddenly this quarters also became available. Very convenient at that time. It had an elevator in it, so that it made it very easy for Mrs. Nimitz.

Q: Well, I want to go on with you then. You told me that during the dinner of the tenth anniversary that he was discussing the Pearl Harbor time, so I know you have some interesting things to tell about that.

Mrs. B.: I don't know the exact date that he left Washington. He was called upon to go out to the Pacific.

Q: Did he tell you anything about how he happened to be selected for the job?

Mrs. B.: No. I'm not certain that he knew, but he was selected so he asked for a couple of things. First, that he would go to the West Coast by train.

Q: Do you know why?

Mrs. B.: He wanted some time, and he said he was tired and he knew he had a big job out there, and he wanted a chance to collect his feelings and his thoughts and plan ahead a bit, and he knew he would be very busy once he got to the West

Coast and then on out. The second request was that his train tickets would not be under his own name. I've forgotten the name he used. It was a simple name - Smith or Walker or Green, or something like that. But he went out and he said nobody was to know him - who he was on the train.

Q: Who went with him, do you know?

Mrs. B.: To my knowledge, he went alone on the train.

Q: It doesn't sound likely, though.

Mrs. B.: Well, a man who wants time to himself, who could stay in his own little room on the train.

Q: Do you know what accommodations did he have on the train?

Mrs. B.: Obviously, it was a private bedroom and stateroom of some sort. I don't know. But he did go out that way, and I believe he went in civilian dress, but I'm not certain. He didn't want any attention called to the fact he was going out, and he wanted to be by himself during that time.

Q: Then how did he get from - where did he come in to, San Francisco?

Mrs. B.: I would - well, probably, Oakland. I don't know whether he flew - I imagine he flew from there on out, but this was one thing he did request. It impressed me, since this was the way he wanted it.

Q: Did he discuss anything further with you that night?

Mrs. B.: Well, people were asking questions of all such things, but I can't recall specifically what they were, but this was one of the things I do remember because it impressed me.

Q: Did he tell you how he felt when they selected him for the job?

Mrs. B.: No. When I was stationed in Pearl Harbor, I saw him out there.

Q: Oh, tell me about that.

Mrs. B.: It was up at Macalapa at the senior officers' swimming pool, and my husband had said, and his family - of course, they'd known him for so many years, if you ever see him introduce yourself. Well, you just don't go up to his office and say, here I am, I know Ed. So, he was swimming and I was going to get up and speak to him then. By the time I could get off my feet he had started across the pool. He was quite a swimmer, and he was out and gone. Years later I told him that I'd seen him there that day, and he said, "Why didn't you speak to me?" Many times out there I was called upon to escort a lady to functions when he was at Pearl Harbor. He said, "If I'd only known you were there, naturally, it would

Mr. and Mrs. Brewer - 42

have been for me to ~~, you know.~~ "have you go with me."

Q: Sure. Wouldn't it have been nice for you?

Mrs. B.: No.

Q: Why not?

Mrs. B.: Because there was feeling amongst the WAVEs, some of them, who were small-minded, I felt - WAVE officers who worked and lived in the BOQ, that any time a WAVE, a junior officer, went out with a senior officer, if you got any kind of special privileges, or they would be deemed to be special privileges, it was because you were dating the brass, and it would have been very inconvenient to have gone out with the Fleet Admiral ~~several times~~.

Q: Oh, I suppose, but I'm afraid I would have put that on my really unimportant side, if I'd had the opportunity to go with him.

Mrs. B.: Yes, but I feel that you still had to live with the people with whom you were working. They could have made it pretty rough and sticky for you.

Q: Unfortunate, isn't it, miserable?

Mrs. B.: Yes. I know occasionally I did go out with a captain and have been at Admirals' parties, and it was just unfortunate.

Q: What was Admiral Nimitz' reaction to WAVES, do you know?

Mrs. B.: I think it was very favorable once he got used to

them.

Q: Tell me about before he got used to them.

Mrs. B.: I'm not sure. He always spoke very highly of the job they were doing and what they were doing.

Q: What year were you in Pearl?

Mrs. B.: I went out in May of '45, and came back in January of '46.

Q: Did you ever get any reaction that he hadn't liked women in the Navy or?

Mrs. B.: No, no.. I never got any reaction from him nor any of the others - high ranking Navy officers.

Q: I did! When they first assigned me in Bremerton, I was the first WAVE there and the Admiral took me down in his private car, which I thought happened to everybody, and - Admiral Sherry, and he said, "I'm giving you to this officer because he's the only officer on the base who said he didn't want WAVEs. So I'm going to teach him a lesson."

Mrs. B.: A very close friend of my father's was a man like that. His reaction was he didn't want women, but as soon as he got one he said, "Boy, she's doing the work of two or three men. Give me more."

Q: I already thought the smarter the man was, the more he appreciated smart people working for him, whether they're women or men. And I think the selection of WAVEs was special.

Mrs. B.: Yes, and every WAVE that was there was there because she wanted to be, whereas some of your men were drafted.

Q: Tell me now about some of the stories that you know that Admiral Nimitz may have related.

Mrs. B.: I can't remember specific stories, unfortunately. I remember one cartoon. Every time we went to see him, of course, he was always giving us a paper or some little thing, it seemed. This was in subsequent years when we were - we'd see them once a year or so, and I remember one cartoon he gave us, which shows...

Q: Which you've given to me and which I'm going to send in.

Mrs. B.: Just get it back to us. It shows a rather high ranking officer looking very gruff, facing an enlisted man in typical enlisted clothes except his trousers are on backwards, and the comment is underneath, "I don't give a dam if you took twenty pills. Put those pants on right."

Q: Cute! I thought he was making an inspection, perhaps, but it's not that important. It's a man of some importance and - it's a commodore, as it happens. I'm going to have a picture made of this. Would you rather have the picture made so that you won't lose it?

Mrs. B.: Oh, no. You have our address.

Q: Yes, I sure do.

Mrs. B.: I remember one Christmas when we came up to visit them.

Mr. and Mrs. Brewer - 45

It was about a month and a half before he died, and he was at his quarters on Goat Island, Quarters No. 1, and we stopped in to see him, not knowing whether we'd actually be able to see him because we'd heard he was quite ill, and he was allowed to have, I believe it was two visitors at a time for a very short time. So Mrs. Nimitz went up to see if it would be all right if - if he would like to see us. He was then limited basically to the second floor, and he said, "None of this two at a time. I know the Brewers as a family. I want to see them all." This is the sort of thing he would do.

Q: Describe that visit. I think it would be interesting.

Mrs. B.: Well, we didn't stay very long with him, of course. We chatted with Mrs. Nimitz a bit, but it was very apparent he was failing.

Q: Set the stage so that I can visualize.

Mrs. B.: He was in a little upstairs sitting room looking towards the Bay Bridge, wasn't it? You could see the traffic going along there because this was below the bridge. And we sat and chatted and he wanted to know how the children were doing and what they were doing.

Q: Where was he? Was he in bed, in a chair?

Mrs. B.: He was in a chair, in a bathrobe, very well groomed.

Q: Seated in a regular chair, not a wheelchair or anything?

Mrs. B.: No it wasn't a wheelchair It was a regular chair.

Mr. and Mrs. Brewer - 46

Q: And were his feet on the floor, or were they propped up?

Mrs. B.: His feet were on the floor.

Cdr. B.: He was wrapped up in a blanket, I think.

Mrs. B.: I think he had a blanket over his knees, but he was in pajamas, bathrobe, and slippers.

Cdr. B.: But he had failed. By that time, he'd already had several strokes, as it turned out, and he had failed quite a bit. I mean, his face was gaunt, of course he had never been full-faced, and he was somewhat articulate, but not too much. You could ask him a question, if it was a simple question, ~~I mean, if it wasn't - so it was rather a - well~~, We were there I wouldn't say more than five minutes, at the most. It was kind of emotion-packed and you could feel that you weren't going to be seeing him much longer.

Mrs. B.: The Christmas before that when we'd seen him, he was in a back brace. He made some sharp remarks, I can't remember specifically what they were, about his corset...

Q: Oh, I wish you could remember.

Mrs. B.: He was talking to you, I think, about that. He always loved to show the children things - the children loved to look at all the things he had - oh, I guess he'd returned the Japanese sword by then.

Cdr. B.: He had all kinds of mementoes, you know, that he'd been given from various commands and ships and so forth, and that's what Midge is referring to...

Q: Yes. Tell me about the Japanese sword you returned. Tell me what you mean by that.

Cdr. B.: Well that was the sword that he was given on the surrender at Tokyo Bay, and he subsequently returned that to the Japanese government.

Q: Oh. It had been given as a token of surrender?

Cdr. B.: Yes. And he in turn...

Q: Did he tell you about that? What prompted him to do it?

Cdr. B.: No - just his decision that after it was all over, this was quite a number of years after, that it rightfully belonged back in the family. The symbol had been transmitted and that was it. But, no, he never expanded on why he did it.

Q: Can you expand a little bit more on the conversation you had on your last Christmas visit.

Mrs. B.: It was basically - he was talking to the children and interested in how we were and said how well we looked, and how nice to see us, and...

Q: Did he comment on how he felt? Nothing about himself?

Mrs. B.: No. We asked, "How are you feeling?" and he said, "Fine, thank you." He wouldn't admit it if he felt poorly. He wouldn't say that.

Q: Apparently he was a man, up until the very last, of excellent health

Mrs. B.: ~~Uh-huh.~~ Yes.

Q: Any more?

Cdr. B.: Can't think of anything else.

Mrs. B.: Well, I know one time that that movie came out and he sent it down for you to show the scout troop. Was it Big Story? Then we also showed it to a group at church. It was a film ~~we~~ he thought would interest us — there's reference to it in one of his letters.

Q: What was it, a Navy film or...?

Mrs. B.: I think it was a Navy film.

Cdr. B.: ~~I can't even...~~

Mrs. B.: It was relatively obscure. I think it was on the Navy.

Q: The Big Story?

Mrs. B.: I believe so.

Q: I have two letters here which are in his handwriting...

Mrs. B.: I have more around some place. I don't know just where.

Q: Would you part with these?

Mr. and Mrs. Brewer - 49

Mrs. B.: If you could have them copied, I'd like to keep them.

Q: 27th February 1956 and 3rd of January 1963. If you don't mind, I'd like to have them copied. I notice the one in '56 that you sent him a horse shoe for his birthday. Is that right?

Mrs. B.: It was a birthday card that had a horse shoe on it. That's what he's referring to.

Q: And he speaks here of having a cold.

Mrs. B.: I think he was slightly susceptible to colds. I know he had pneumonia several times.

Q: That's a nice letter.

Mrs. B.: The letters are always warm.

Q: Oh, yes, he refers in this letter of 3rd of January '63 to a 16-mm. film The Big Story "which I am sure you and the children will enjoy as much as the Boy Scouts." Oh, that's interesting. So he still had interest in the Scouts even at this time?

Mrs. B.: You see, by that time, our son was in scouting.

Q: Is "Tag " your boy?

Mrs. B.: Yes.

Q: What does he mean "an icicle badge".

Mrs. B.: Er, that was - I think I'd written them probably that

Mr. and Mrs. Brewer - 50

they'd gone on one of their monthly camp-outs, and it got cold and the food froze, and those that survived the camp outside got an "icicle badge."

Q: Oh, I see.

Mrs. B.: It was an innovation of the troop.

Q: Well, I think you've given Mr. Potter, our biographer - at least I hope we have given him some items that he hasn't had before, and I don't know whether they would like the original letters or...

Mrs. B.: Well, as long as they come back, it's all I ask.

Q: If they have them, they would want to keep them in their archives.

Mrs. B.: Well, those are personal letters.

Q: I know. So maybe I'll have a picture taken of them and then they'll let you have them. Do you have any pictures of the Admiral?

Mrs. B.: Oh, we have quite a few of the Admiral. They're downstairs.

Cdr. B.: They're all official ones, though, and you could get them.

Mrs. B.: One at his home at Goat Island.

Q: I wondered if you might have any that would be different than the history section of the Navy might have?

Cdr. B.: No, except...

Q: You speak of the Admiral's being a hiker?

Mrs. B.: Oh, he was a great hiker. He had a rather distinctive walk when he went on a hike, and he'd start out with a dog and a cane. I don't know whether the cane was to beat off other dogs or what, but he - well, I think when we first moved on Santa Barbara Road, they had a wire-haired dachshund, but the Admiral would hike much more than the dachshund liked, and half the time the dachshund would show up at home before the Admiral got there. Then something happened - the dog died, and people knew their great love for dogs and I believe the dog came from the Berkeley pound, but it was a full standard poodle, Gigi, and that really gave the Admiral something to walk with because Gigi loved to walk, and Gigi was really very fond of the Admiral. And she was - the dog was with him at the Quarters when he died.

Q: Do you know - that's another aspect that I hadn't heard, speaking of his fondness for animals. Other than dogs, or...?

Mrs. B.: They always had bird feeders and humming birds, ~~he was particularly~~ - he always had a humming bird feeder. In fact, he told us where to get a humming bird feeder, and what to put in. They always had two or three going in the patio there. His garden was always immaculate and the lawn was beautiful. He always maintained that he just did the work and Mrs. Nimitz told him what she wanted done.

Q: Do you know what music he liked?

Mrs. B.: No, not specifically what he liked. They were very fond of the symphony, supported the symphony, but I...

Q: Did they attend it?

Mrs. B.: Yes, and the opera. But I am not positive whose choice it was.

Q: I know that in Pearl, one of the men who lived in his quarters said that he liked symphony and had many symphonic records. But you have no way of knowing his favorite opera or favorite symphony?

Mrs. B.: No, I haven't.

Q: Do you know what his favorite reading material was?

Mrs. B.: He read a great deal, but I think he read - I don't know how much he read in the way of novels, although he was always commenting on various things he'd read, and any article that came up that would be of interest to us, he would always call it to our attention.

Q: So he was a wide reader, then. Did he watch TV a lot?

Mrs. B.: Not too much. I remember one time they were most upset - they had to appear on that Person To Person show. I have some letters...

Q: Edward R. Murrow's show?

Mrs. B.: Yes. They didn't want to do it, but they were asked to do it.

Mr. and Mrs. Brewer - 53

Q: Where was that taken?

Mrs. B.: That was taken down in Santa Barbara. It started out with the Admiral in the front lawn - I guess the pictures were taken from our house - with this sundial he had on the front lawn, which he was a favorite spot for taking pictures with various people that had to have their pictures taken of them with the Admiral, and he would explain it to them.

Q: Let's see now. We've pretty well covered most of the items. Oh, what kind of a bathrobe was he wearing the last day you saw him? What color? Do you remember?

Mrs. B.: I remember it seemed maroon or Navy blue - not a wild one, definitely.

Q: Was it plaid or solid color?

Mrs. B.: I would say solid color.

Q: And your recollection is Navy blue?

Mrs. B.: Navy blue or maroon, it could have been gray. He was not a wild dresser.

Q: Well, that's covered a wide range.

Mrs. B.: I remember he gave my husband and I two pictures of himself. We have them downstairs. The children each have pictures inscribed to them. But he gave us one inscribed to my husband and myself thanking us for our part in the war effort, and the other one is to the four of us. One is front face of him, and the other one is the signing of the peace treaty, and the children are proudest of those.

Q: I do agree with you that he was a wide distributor of photographs because practically everyone with whom one speaks has that picture of him. But it certainly is a marvelous picture to be prized.

This will come back to you, now, and if in the meantime in the middle of the night you suddenly remember, why didn't I tell her that, make a note of it and add it to the manuscript, will you? And especially if you remember any stories. I just love to know stories that people have told..

Mrs. B.: Did you mention about going to the Santa Clara County Fair?

Cdr. B.: Yes.

Mrs. B.: The horse shoes matches, and the Admiral watching them with a child on each knee. It was a very hot day. In fact, you wondered why...

Q: Who all went?

Mrs. B.: Well, the Admiral went, and a couple of the Bahta girls, in his car, and we...

Q: What girls?

Mrs. B.: Bahta girls. These were four Hungarian girls that came over and the Admiral's youngest daughter met them at the Dominican school, and he befriended them and was like a father to them. Their family was still over in Hungary. In fact, he was their sponsor for citizenship.

Q: Now, this is interesting, see, which you didn;t tell me before.

Mrs. B.: I don;t know where this came.

Q: You see.

Mrs. B.: Yes. And we went down there and all had lunch and we visited the live stock

Q: Now, your children...?

Mrs. B.: Our two children - they were about 2 and 4...

Q: And the Bata girls and you...

Mrs. B.: I don!t remember how many of the Bata girls - and one Navy officer, I believe. Cozard drove them down and we met them there.

Q: And you and your husband?

Mrs. B.: Yes, and our two children.

Q: And Mrs. Nimitz?

Mrs. B.: No. She did not go.

Q: OK, now tell me about the day.

Mrs. B.: We went down - he was especially interested because they were having some championship horse shoe pitching and, knowing my husband's interest in horse shoe pitching, why, we

Mr. and Mrs. Brewer - 56

went down. And after lunch and touring the animals and livestock of the country fair, we went to see these matches, which - well, it was just ringer after ringer after ringer. It was almost boring. But there were pictures taken of the Admiral and there he is watching these matches with one child on each knee.

Q: Now, who has those pictures?

Mrs. B.: I don't know. They were pictures taken by papers, I believe.

Q: I see. And what year was this?

Mrs. B.: Oh, it would be early - late - summer '53, I would believe.

Q: And what was he wearing that day?

Mrs. B.: Sport coat, shirt, and slacks.

Q: Did he take his jacket off when it became so terribly hot?

Mrs. B.: Probably.

Cdr. B.: He favored flannel _slacks_.

Mrs. B.: Well, he liked gray flannel troussers, too, and a tweed coat, which was a very common thing....

Q: Now, tell me more about his sponsoring the Bata girls? This is B-a-t-a, like the shoe company, from Hungary?

Mrs. B.: I don't remember how it is spelled, but I think Mary, who is about 15 years younger than the three older children, and she was at Dominican in high school, and she met these girls then, as I understand the story, and they had been brought over to this country through - their father got them out of Hungary and they got into Switzerland...

Q: Were they Jewish?

Mrs. B.: I don't believe so. I think they were Roman Catholics. And, into Switzerland and then on over to this country, and they came up for citizenship and the Admiral was their sponsor.

Q: That's interesting. Was he a religious man or do you have any way of knowing?

Mrs. B.: He was not too religious. He had a religion within himself, but I don't think he was a churchgoer.

Q: Did you ever hear him express his philosophy on it - life after death or whether there was any? Do you know if he believed in it?

Mrs. B.: No., I don't.

Q: He was too busy living this one, I guess, to worry about...

Mrs. B.: I think he was at peace with himself.

Q: When he was so ill at the last, why, there was no indication of disturbance or disquiet on his part?

Mrs. B.: Not that I know of.

Q: She's shaking her head, saying no.

Q: Well, should we terminate this? Each time we do, though, you think of something else and that's why I say if you start generating ideas, why, don't hesitate to keep a note of them so you can add them.

INDEX

for an interview

with

MR. AND MRS. EDWARD V. BREWER

Aquinas, Sister Mary (Nimitz) 56-57

Battha family, 54-56

Berkeley, 1, 4-6, 9-15, 23, 28-29, 51

Birmingham, 2-3, 21

Bougainville, 3

California, University of, 1, 4

Canaga, Captain Bruce L., 15

Cozard, George E., 37, 55

Ewa, 6

Exercises, 14

Goat Island, 38, 45, 50

Horse shoes, 5-6

MacArthur, General Douglas, 37

Mare Island, 4, 21

Nimitz, Mrs. Chester W., 4-5, 10, 13, 23, 28-34, 37-38

Nimitz, Mary - see Aquinas

Nimitz, Nancy, 13-14

NROTC, 1, 11

Pearl Harbor, 2-3, 6, 21, 35, 39, 41, 43

San Francisco, 25, 40

San Francisco Chronicle, 3

Santa Monica, 18-19, 22

Santa Monica Evening Outlook, 22

Tarawa, 4

Tokyo Bay, 47

Wake, 2

WAVES, 35, 42-44

West Point, 34

DECLARATION OF TRUST

The undersigned does hereby appoint and designate as his (her) Trustee herein, the Secretary-Treasurer and Publisher of the United States Naval Institute to perform and discharge the following duties, powers, and privileges in connection with the possession and use of a certain taped interview between the undersigned and the Oral History Department of the United States Naval Institute.

(1) As an <u>Open</u> transcript it may be read (or the tape audited) by qualified researchers upon presentation of proper credentials as determined by the Trustee. In the case of interviews about the late Fleet Admiral C. W. Nimitz, it is intended that first use of the material shall be made by the biographer of the Fleet Admiral, Professor E. B. Potter, and the Naval Institute is authorized to deal with the material in this fashion.

(2) It is expressly understood that in giving this authorization, I am in no way precluded from placing such restrictions as I may desire upon use of the interview at any time during my lifetime, nor does this authorization in any way affect my rights to the copyright of any literary expressions that may be contained in the interview.

Witness my hand and seal this __5th__ day of __March__ 19__70__

George E. Cogard

I hereby accept and consent to the foregoing Declaration of Trust and the powers therein conferred upon me as Trustee.

R. E. Bowker
Secretary-Treasurer and Publisher

Interview with George E. Cozard, Public Relations Representative
of the Pacific Gas and Electric Company
At: His home, 1093 Francisco Street, San Francisco
Subject: Fleet Admiral Chester W. Nimitz
Date: 24 January 1970
By: Etta Belle Kitchen

Q: My only introduction is to start Mr. Cozard off by asking him how he happened to know Admiral Nimitz, and from then on he has a series of extremely interesting reminiscences about the Admiral.

Mr. C.: When I was stationed at the Naval Gun Factory in Washington, D. C., and had charge of the gate guard there, I got to know quite a few of the people who were on Admiral King's flagship and ...

Q: Ernie King?

Mr. C.: Yes. He was Chief of Naval Operations at that time, and Admiral Nimitz took over the job from Admiral King. There was a young fellow there who drove Admiral Nimitz, and they used to keep their car in the Naval Gun Factory garage. I knew this fellow fairly well because, at that time, I was trying to get my private pilot's licence, and we both were doing the same thing. We were flying out of the old Congressional Airport at Rockville, Maryland. This man's name was Robert Lee, which kind of sticks in your head - Robert M. Lee. Bob had worked for United Airlines for a good many years before the second war, and he was serving a four-year enlistment in the Marine Corps, and he wanted to go back to United Airlines. He liked his job with Admiral Nimitz, but he thought if he reenlisted in the Marine Corps he might get sent overseas or something and get farther and farther away from his career. So he told me that the Admiral wanted someone to take his place, and he asked me if I'd like to be interviewed, and between Bob and myself we went down to see Admiral Nimitz.

Q: What year was that?

Mr. C.: About 1946 - early '46, probably about January or February. The Admiral took over, I think, in about December '45, because his term ended in December of '47 - it was a two-year term. And we went down to see the Admiral. I went in for an interview with him in the middle of one afternoon; the Admiral asked me where I'd been in the Marine Corps and I told him. He asked me how I was doing, and he asked me if I'd like to work for him, and I said yes. He said, "Well, I'll tell you what. Why don't you just wait around and drive me home today." So I stuck around with Bob in his office and when the Admiral was through - and he worked very long hours there - along about 7 o'clock or so I drove him home. He lived at the Naval Observatory, Quarters A, I think it was. He said "Pick me up tomorrow morning," then I took the car back to the Naval Gun Factory garage.

Usually he would leave his house about 7:15 - 7:30 at the latest, and I arrived there about 7 o'clock. At that time, he had two people driving him, Daniel McCarthy and Bob Lee, and he had two orderlies in the office. The drivers worked very long hours, and they were supposed to alternate - a day on and a day off. They picked the Admiral up in the morning about 7:15, he often worked at the office quite late, then he might go to a reception in the evening, and possibly a dinner, and by the time the driver got through for the night, it would be one or two o'clock in the morning. So they alternated their days of working.

Anyway, I put the car away at the Gun Factory, then went back the next morning to pick up the Admiral, and took him down to the office, and stuck around all day. It wasn't till about two days later, I think, that I told my Commanding Officer what I was up to - that I'd been working for Admiral Nimitz without being transferred to his staff. So I was then assigned to Marine Corps Headquarters for administrative purposes; my records were kept at Marine Headquarters, and I worked for the CNO's office. I worked for a long period of time as the driver, a day on and a day off. McCarthy had quite a few personal and health problems, so the Admiral just started getting me to drive him everywhere, and the first thing you know I was working continuously for him. I said to him one day, "Admiral, do you know what they call this type of duty? They call this 'day on and stay on.'" He thought it was a big thing, and a lot of times when he had people come to town he'd recite this to them. He'd introduce me to all of them and say, "He's working day on and stay on."

Q: Did he say anything when you said that the first time?

Mr. C.: He thought it was very funny, because, as I say, he worked long hours.

Q: And he expected everyone else to.

Mr. C.: Yes. Ordinarily if nothing else was scheduled, he would work till about seven in the evening in his office. Saturday, well, we'd go down to the office about eight in the morning and stay till about maybe mid-afternoon.

Q; His office, then, was in the Pentagon?

Mr. C.: No, it was at 18th and Constitution, the old Navy building. He never did work out of the Pentagon. When Admiral Denfeld relieved Admiral Nimitz the office then was moved to the Pentagon.

And Sunday, quite often he'd go to the office; just the Admiral and I would be there. It was a very short day for us. We'd go to the office about ten in the morning and only stay till about two in the afternoon.

Q: Well, you really didn't have much life of your own, then, did you?

Mr. C.: No. I spent quite a bit of time with him.

Q: I think it's important to know what the Admiral's activities were, and I think for a biographer, he would like to know his daily routine, which you've given me as far as working hours are concerned

Mr. C.: Right. Quite often he wouldn't want to ride all the way to the office. We would drive down - these things are hard to remember now from a distance, 1946 was quite a few years ago. - Massachusetts Avenue, and down through Rock Creek Park, and part the way down through the park - I don't know what section it was exactly, I'd stop and the Admiral would get out and he would walk the rest of the way to the office.

Q: That's a long hike.

Mr. C.: It's a long hike. Then I would drive on down, go to the office and be there when he got there. He was very much concerned with physical fitness and keeping in good condition. At that time he was still smoking.

Q: Was he?

Mr. C.: Yes. He smoked Chesterfields. I'd go out and buy him cigarettes, and like a lot of great men I have known some mechanical things just threw him for a loop. He always had trouble with his cigarette lighter. I'd take his cigarette lighter apart from time to time, put a new flint in it, or make sure that there was enough fluid. Quite often he'd say his cigarette lighter wouldn't work, and it was my chore to try to straighten things out. It kind of baffled him. He autographed pictures for people, many, many pictures over the years. We had a whole collection of pictures in a supply cabinet. In one of the pictures he was in his blues with his hand - his elbow on a desk and his hand up at 45-degree angle with a cigarette in his hand, and I don't recall after he stopped smoking ever using that picture again. Up until that time I think he used it, and after that he never wanted to use that picture. I think until the time I left we had a supply of those on hand. It was probably about 1947 or so when he decided to quit smoking, and that was it.

Q: Do you know what prompted him to stop?

Mr. C.: No. I think it was just a matter of pride, sort of mastering his own fate, and looking after his health. And when he made up his mind to do something he did it. He just decided that, by God, he was going to stop smoking cigarettes, and he stopped.

Q: Did you observe his activities during the day?

Mr. C.: Quite often. When he moved around Washington, D. C., if he went up to the Capitol, the White House, or to one of the office buildings for meetings, or over to the Pentagon to meet with General Eisenhower, or anywhere else, usually I took him. I say, "took him" - I drove the car. And so after I'd gotten to the office in the morning I had duty to do in those days as sort of an orderly and messenger and escort for guests, yet I kept pretty close track of his daily schedule because when he had to move outside the building usually I was driving the car and taking him.

Q: Was he a man of routine?

Mr. C.: Yes, to a great extent, he was. He kept his life, even though it was sort of an unregulated life, he tried to keep it regulated as far as some of his activities went - I told you he was very much concerned with staying in good condition. He couldn't stand to be ill or to feel that he was slipping out of shape. He was very much concerned with being healthy and enjoying life. He had several little personal habits - for a long time he wore detachable collars on his shirts. Apparently they did this in the old days quite a bit - I wasn't around then, I was a youngster. And he had a couple of favorite old spots in Washington where he bought detachable collars. I don't remember now, yes, they were paper collars. He wore them on one side, turned them over, and, you know, wore them, and threw them away.

Q: This was when he was in uniform?

Mr. C.: Uh-huh. And I used to go and buy detachable collars for him - that was one of my chores. And he had little things he wanted - certain ways he wanted his uniform pressed, I remember that. We all have that, though, I'm sure. He was pretty human. He was very kind, very considerate. He had time for everybody, and even when we were going from one place to another one he was always kind enough to offer a ride to someone. He was very courteous. His manners were most courtly as far as women were concerned, whether you were a scrubbing lady or a diplomat's wife, he treated you with the same amount of courtesy and respect.

Q: Do you have a "for instance" on that, by the way?

Mr. C.: Well, no, I can't think of any particular one. He always stood when a lady came into the room, and he always made sure that his own wife was seated in the car and looked after before he got in. He was kind to children - there were a lot of children. There was one little girl in Iowa, I believe, who wrote to the Admiral starting when she was a little girl, and she wrote to him and invited him to her farm, and all of her letters told him about her farm life and what she was doing, her daily activities, and he answered her and senther little things.

Q: He didn't know her?

Mr. C.: No. Even when she finally grew up, many years later, and became a mother, she sill corresponded and sent pictures of her children. He didn't know her, except through their correspondence. He was this way with someone he'd never met. He was always kind and considerate. He had certain ideas quite often about items he desired. One time he sent me out on a search for some bread like he used to get in New England in the old days, and I don't think anybody still made bread like that. I can't remember exactly what the brand was. He described it to me, and I went round to different bakeries and stores searching for it, and I never could find it. He had the idea, you know, that there was someone around who still baked that type, and if we looked around we could find it

Q; Did he get mad when you didn't find it?

Mr. C.: No, no. He would lose his temper now and then, but he wasn't the type of man to really lose his temper and yell and make a big fuss, but every now and then when it was deserved - you could feel it. He'd sort of just stiffen up a little bit and he'd look at you with those piercing blue eyes, and you'd know that you'd gone too far, or that something had upset him.

Q: Can you give me a "for instance" of when he got mad?

Mr. C.: No, I can't think of any particular time. I remember several times talking to him and saying or doing things - being young and brash then - there were a few times that I got him a little bit irritated. I used to drive him very fast on some of our trips. We used to take trips to Philadelphia and other cities, and I used to drive fairly fast. There wasn't as much traffic on the roads as there is today. A lot of times we'd have a police escort, and the police would meet us at segments of the highway and we'd move along very fast. Now and then I'd be driving along the highway, and I'd be going at a pretty good clip, then I'd slow down to about 65 for awhile. He'd look at his watch and say, "Listen, we're in a hurry. Now speed up, but stay within the law."

Q: And you stayed within the law?

Mr. C.: I'd say, "Okay." Once or twice when we were driving to some engagement - I remember one night, it was a foggy night, and he started telling me to slow down and to watch it, and I said, "Admiral, listen, I'm in this car, too, you know, and I don't want to get killed any more than you do. So why not just knock it off," sort of in that tone. And Mrs. Nimitz thought it was very funny.

Q: Did you use those precise words?

Mr. C.: Yes, I think so. And then I thought, "Oh, God, I've gone too far this time with him," even though our relationship was unusual - over a period of years - it developed into something that was quite unique.

Q: Well, to tell an Admiral to "knock it off!" Did you really say those words?

Mr. C.: Yes, I believe that was what I said, or very close to it. And afterwards I could have bitten my tongue, but it was too late then.

Q: Wll, I'm sure you were both rather tense with emotion because there was a certain amount of danger?

Mr. C.: But he was a gentleman.

He had little routines - you asked if he followed routines. He looked at his watch as often as a railroad conductor - he timed things. We had to arrive at places when we were scheduled to arrive on time, which made it a little bit rough on me. I think if I'd been the type of person to develop an ulcer I'd have had one. After a period of time together, when we had settled down to a routine, when we got to know each other, then he would just tell me where he was going and ask me what time we should leave. When I first went to work for him he had a complete staff, and later as the years went by, the staff dwindled. He let people go from time to time, and he got down to the point where I was the only one working with him.

Slowly I started to handle all the chores. I answered the correspondence, I replied to invitations to people wanting him to come and ...

Q: Are we getting ahead of ourselves a little bit?

Mr. C.: We might be.

Q: Yes, because I want to cover each of the phases. At the moment we're still when he's CNO.

Mr. C.: Right. We got to the point where he was asking me what time we should leave to get to places, and then he would time his departure accordingly. I would bring the car up to the side door of the Navy Department, or his house, or wherever we were staying at the time, and he would appear on schedule - at the scheduled departure time. Then it was up to me to get us to where we were going, and arrive on time. He wanted to arrive exactly on time, and he didn't mean for us to be two minutes early because that was equally as bad in his estimation as being two minutes late, as far as the host and hostess went, and ...

Q: Was this true socially as well as professionally?

Mr. C.: Yes, in everything. He would look at his watch and say, "Well, it's now five until (whatever it was, five til seven for example), and we should be right on time." And I'd either speed up or slow down accordingly. A lot of times, we would almost get to a place, even a social event, and I'd say, "Is it all right if I go around this way. It's a little bit longer but we have five minutes to kill, and he'd say, "Fine." We tried to arrive every place right on time, and did for years. Well, one time I drove him to the Army and Navy game. Now it must have been in 1946 or 1947. It was in November 1946. With the Admiral and Mrs. Nimitz were his aide at the time, Commander Fluckey and Mrs. Fluckey, and President and Mrs. Sproul of the University of California. We had an old limousine - a 1941 Packard limousine. It was a beautiful old thing. It was like a magnificent tank, but it ran beautifully on the highway. And we all went up to the Army and Navy game in it, we ate boxed lunches on the way and left two or three boxed lunches in the car. Then after the Army and Navy game we all got into the car. I think we might have gone over to the Navy Yard for a while, but when we got in the car to leave and head back to the Admiral's quarters at the Observatory, the Admiral looked at his watch and he said to everybody, "Well, it's now exactly eight o'clock and we'll pull up in front of our house at five after eleven." So I took my cue and I thought it was really up to me to show how we operated, because as I said we did operate on schedule. How we did it for all those years though I'll never know. But we operated on schedule, and so I got on the old Packard throttle and figured - okay, I'll make really good time the first part of the journey, and then I can always slow down a little bit toward the end and nobody will know the difference. And so we were going down the road and I was pushing along hot and heavy until we were somewhere around Bainbridge, Maryland, then everything went fluey. I think I must have burnt out half the connecting rod bearings in the car. There was this terrible racket from the engine compartment. I think Commander Fluckey's wife was sitting in the front - the middle of the front. And so I took my foot off and gas pedal and put it back down again, and I said to her, "I think I hear a noise," and she said, "Yes, I do too, and my feet are getting hot." I had blown up the engine in the middle of the country, and the middle of the night.

Q: How fast had you been going?

Mr. C.: I'd been going maybe 85, 90.

Q: Not really?

Mr. C.: Yes, somewhere around there. So I pulled in to the next service station we came to, and the guy running the station crawled under the car. It was too big to go on his grease rack. He crawled under the car and looked around, checked the oil, checked the water, couldn't find anything wrong. Several of the people were hungry, so we broke out the boxed lunches we had left, and began eating the apples. We decided that Bainbridge wasn't too far off, so we'd continue there, and see if they'd give us another car. We limped down the highway and pulled in to Bainbridge. And you can imagine pulling in with this group in a limousine with five stars on it at something like midnight would be terrifying. The guards acted as if they couldn't believe it at the gate, and the clanking engine kind of terrified me. There were lots of running in circles and lights flashing, and people acting very confused. I think the Admiral rolled down his window, and his wife said something like, "Please don't cough. You'll have half the barracks up." They finally got a couple of cars for us and provided another driver.

We split our groups up, and started out of Bainbridge. I got down the road a few miles and looked down and - I couldn't believe it - in their big hurry to give us cars they gave me a car that was almost out of gas. We had to stop at a service station, so I think that by the time we pulled up in front of the Admiral's house at the Observatory it was about 2:30 in the morning. I never said a word to him about the schedule or about our arriving back at five after eleven, and I don't think he ever mentioned it either. I think that was about the only time that we didn't make it at the scheduled time.

Q: Was he upset? Was he mad?

Mr. C.: No, no, I don't think so. I think he would like to have had us arrive at the time he said we were going to arrive. That would have been very nice, and would have kept our record intact.

Q: And how long were you in Washington with him?

Mr. C.: From 1946 through 1947 until he retired, or gave up the CNO's position. He never really retired. However, that was his last command. I think in his own mind he couldn't quite decide which place he wanted to go when he left Washington. Mrs. Nimitz lived out here on the West Coast during the Second War - in Berkeley. And the Admiral was, of course, born in Texas. Once or twice during the final part of his tour as CNO he asked me, he said, "How'd you like to be a cowboy?" And I said, "That'd be great. I'd like to live on a ranch and how really wild I thought it would be." Several times I asked him if he had room for me, or if he was going to maintain an office, and he said, - no, he was not going to maintain a

Cozard - 15

staff. He was always concerned about manpower and saving the Navy's funds. So I stayed on with Admiral Denfeld when he came in as Chief of Naval Operations. I stayed there up until, oh, I guess I was on that job for about - possibly - a year, maybe a year and a half.

Q: After Admiral Nimitz left?

Mr. C.: After he left, yes. Then one of the officers on the staff - I've forgotten which one now - was on the West Coast and saw the Admiral. When he came back to Washington he said, "The Admiral asked me if you'd like to come out and work with him."

Q: Now, was he retired then?

Mr. C.: No, he didn't have an active command then. He was living in Berkeley and had an office in the Federal Office Building in San Francisco.

Q: But he had - his last active duty when he was still CNO, and then came back and lived in Berkeley in his private home?

Mr. C.: Yes. His title then was Special Assistant to the Secretary of the Navy. He covered a lot of speaking engagements, and, I'm not quite sure but I think he was on Selection Boards and things of this nature. We've got pretty far afield from the Admiral, and the things that happened in Washington. I remember one trip we made to Philadelphia. He saw a bar that said "Ship Ahoy" or some such thing on it, and he said, "We'll stop there on our way back. That probably belongs to some old seaman, and maybe we should stop and have a beer." And the rest of the group with us talked him out of it. It was kind of a rough neighborhood, and probably the bar didn't belong to an old seaman, but he was intrigued with the name.

Q: That's cute.

Mr. C.: He had a very quick mind and was interested in everything that was going on. He looked out, as we traveled, and observed everything. When we crossed a bridge he sometimes wondered exactly how long the bridge was, or how this place got its name, or why this happened, and how this was related to that. His brain was very active.

Q: He was thinking all the time?

Mr. C.: All the time. He was a very, very sweet man, a very gentle man, very kind.

Q: Now, before we leave Washington, do you remember any other incidents? Was he there at the time of the Unification Act? I've forgotten the date, but I think it was 1947.

Mr. C.: I can't remember that either exactly. I'm pretty sure that he was though.

Q: Do you remember how he felt on that?

Mr. C.: No. He never really did express himself on it to me. I could some times feel as an old Navy man how he felt on issues. The Admiral was a dedicated Navy man.

Q: And he felt - am I judging correctly - he was opposed to it?

Mr. C.: I believe so. I would say, yes.

Q: You did not hear him say any specific words?

Mr. C.: No.

Q: And I'm sure he was too wise to make any public comments about it?

Mr. C.: Now and then he would voice his opinion on an issue.

Q: Do you remember any?

Mr. C.: No, not particularly now. If we had something, some particular instance that triggered my memory, we may come up with some of these things.

Q: That's the issue I recall, with the Air Force attempting to take over and — that's the way I'd phrase it — and the conflict between the bombers and the carriers and so on. I think you referred to a B-36 ...

Mr. C.: That was later, when I was out here in California. There were lots of meetings that took place down at the Naval Line School. I think Admiral Nimitz was out of town at that time, and I was sent down there with a group of sailors and provided a motor pool to transport a lot of the members at the meeting.

Q: But that didn't relate actually to Admiral Nimitz?

Mr. C.: No. It was something entirely different.

Q: Do you remember any other incidents that are noteworthy during the time he was CNO? I think you've given a good picture of that period and his days and his promptness. All of those are interesting.

Mr. C.: I'd like to go back, if I could, in my own mind and reconstruct month by month the things that we did. During that time, of course, I got to know all the members of his family. They are really an amazing family. One time, many years later – this is out of context, but – the Admiral and I used to go for walks in the Berkeley hills when he was getting along in years. He'd walk along – he gave me a cane that belonged to, I think, General MacArthur – and we'd carry our canes with us as we walked. I used mine to hit rocks and to point to things. We would go for walks up through the hills and look for wild life. What he was doing in part really was just his usual thing, staying in shape, that he'd been doing for years. He did exercises every morning to stay in good physical condition. We were walking along one day and we came to a point where we'd stop now and then, just about the time when we thought the Admiral needed a break, but we never said that. We would stop to examine a rock or, now and then, we'd stop to look off in the distance. I could figure just about the point where he was getting a little bit tired and needed a little pause, and so we'd stop for some reason. It wouldn't do for us to stop because the Admiral needed a little rest. So, one day we were walking along and we stopped and we were kind of gazing out toward the bay, and he said, "You know, every man needs the companionship of a good woman." That was all. There was nothing more said, and we resumed our walk. It was never mentioned again.

I remember when we were in Washington Mrs. Nimitz took part in a lot of the social events in the capital. They had a dog at that time. They always had a dog during the time that I knew them. The dog was a cocker spaniel whose name was Freckles. Mrs. Nimitz is an artist, a gourmet cook, and a remarkable woman.

Q: A beautiful woman, too!

Mr. C.: Oh, a beautiful woman, simply a remarkable woman. She played the piano and when she played one particular song Freckles would jump up on the piano bench and howl like crazy, and it almost got to the point where he was howling in time to the music. She went to several places and put on a little show with Freckles; I can't remember but I believe it was for charity. She would play the piano and Freckles would howl away, and he would stand for the audience.

Q: What did the Admiral think of that?

Mr. C.: Oh, he thought that was really great, priceless.

Q: He got a kick out of it?

Mr. C.: On his walks there in Washington Freckles would accompany him. Much later on, in California, he had a little wire-haired dachshund named Dyna, who didn't pay any attention to rank at all, and instead of plodding along with the Admiral would run off in the bushes. So half the time was spent hunting for Dyna rather than walking.

The Admiral was a great horse shoe pitcher. He pitched horse shoes when he was CHief of Naval Operations; on at least one occasion he pitched with President Truman. He had one or two favorite trick horse-shoe pitchers who used to appear now and then and do tricks, either at his place or the White House.

Q: And then when you left - I don't want to stop you, now, if there are any more recollections of Washington, but you spoke them of coming out to be with him here - here being Berkeley.

Mr. C.: Yes, I spoke of here, being Berkeley. There are many, many things in Washington I could possibly think of, but they'll probably come back to me later. That was, you know the really active part of - the end of his really active naval service.

Q: Then when he went out of active service, he was entitled to take how many people with him?

Mr. C.: He was entitled, I think, to about eight. He had an aide, a secretary, a driver, and stewards - I think about eight altogether I wanted to tell you one other thing that happened to come to mind, very minor but just to show you he was human. When we'd make a trip some place he didn't like to carry a big pencil in his pocket. He carried a small stub of a pencil. I'd quite often break a pencil in half and sharpen half of it so that he had a short pencil to carry with him.

Q: Why was that? Because it made a hole in his pocket?

Mr. C.: Possibly so. He disliked carrying a big pencil. So,

when we started out some place I'd break off a pencil, sharpen it, and he'd carry a stub of a pencil with him. And it was just one of the little things that was part of Admiral Nimitz. He also like to travel light - quite often he made short trips with a razor and toothbrush in his pocket.

Q: I know he had a fantastic memory for people and places and important dates. Did he have this perfect memory for events as well as people?

Mr. C.: Oh, yes. He could remember people and associate people with places. Many times he would tell me stories about the early days in the Navy. And once or twice when the Admiral was with some of the old timers he'd forget - I was around so much they'd think I was part of their group - they would talk about these things as if I was there and remembered it myself. After a while I got so I remembered who was who, and what time they were there, and what had happened at that particular time, even though I was a child when the events took place.

Q: Did he tell you about Pearl Harbor, and how he was selected, and how he felt at the time - any of those recollections?

Mr. C.: He talked about it, and he talked about when he arrived there, the conditions he found, and the tremendous job he knew he had ahead of him. I don't think he could even imagine when he was in Washington, D. C. before he headed out to Pearl Harbor what to expect, but he wasn't quite prepared for what he found.

Q: The devastation, you mean?

Mr. C.: Yes.

Q: And the morale — did he ever mention the morale?

Mr. C.: He mentioned it. However, he didn't dwell on the morale.

Q: And then instead of taking eight people into retirement with him, he took how many?

Mr. C.: When he came to California and set up an office, he had a secretary, an aide, and a driver.

Q: Where was his office?

Mr. C.: His office was in the Federal Building. That was his whole staff. He did have the services of the Commandant of the 12th Naval District in the same building, and he did have the services of some of the other people. There was a Navy Public Information Office, and there were several people who could offer services to him.

I happened to think of something — when we come back to it. When I first went to work for him in Washington of course my main job was driving for him, and then I slowly took on other duties.

Q: This was still when you were in Washington?

Mr. C.: In Washington, yes. Then I got sort of involved with the whole family. I know the family, and know relatives, like I know my own family. We finally got to the point where the Admiral would have anybody else drive him except me, perhaps because we always kept our time schedule and he could depend on me. One morning when we were in Washington - I hope you don't mind me going back ...

Q: No, of course not.

Mr. C.: One morning when we were in Washington and I'd been working for him for maybe eight months I didn't show up. I was sick with something, I don't recall exactly, but I couldn't make it to work. So half an hour or so before I was supposed to pick him up I called the office and said I thought I'd be late. And then I called back later on and said, "Listen, I'm not going to make it at all today, I'm sick." I didn't show up at his house and he waited, instead of calling or trying to get another ride, or calling the office and asking for another car to be sent for him he waited. He insisted that I would show up. He waited for about half an hour, which was very unlike him at that point, because he figured that I would show up, that there was something - maybe I'd had a flat tire of something unavoidable. He waited outside on the porch.

Q: He knew you'd be there!

Mr. C.: He figured I'd show up.

We got to the point where I took him around every day. Then I started to go on trips with him when he flew into different cities; we'd pick up a car at the airport and I would drive. In most places there was a police escort or a guide car or somebody to point the way. You can imagine flying in to some strange city, and starting to drive around, and find your way, and stay on schedule. I drove him around in quite a few towns and cities. He used to tell people that I'd worked for him for many years, and that I know my way around in every city in the United States. I often wondered what would happen if I was left to my own devices. We'd probably just go round in circles.

Q: And then when you came out here did he give up his office in the Federal Building?

Mr. C.: No, he kept his office. He had his office right up till the end.

When I came out to serve with him he had an aide, a secretary, and I used to stay in the office when he didn't need transportation I would go to Berkeley and pick him up, a good many of his engagement were in San Francisco - social engagements and civic functions.

Q: And he still set a daily schedule?

Mr. C.: He would keep a certain amount of a daily schedule. I would take the mail to his house, and get his signature on the things that had been typed, and receive instructions from him, and now and then he'd come in to the office. I think he figured when he came in to the office he was kind of trapped, and he had a hard time getting away. He answered a lot of his correspondence by long hand. I would imagine there are quite a few people in the country who have letters from him.

Q: Yes, and you have some nice ones that I want to take, if I may?

Mr. C.: Okay. He autographed quite a few pictures. Certain pictures were his favorites for people that had served in the Pacific - he had a standard inscription. He would say, "To so and so, with great appreciation for your contribution to the war effort which made possible the above scene," and sign his name. On the picture where the surrender document was he would sign his name again. These made very very nice treasures for people. He was very fond of children; he took a lot of time and a great deal of pains to make certain children received the proper attention. We had a small surrender picture and a small picture of the Admiral in his blues that we called children-sized pictures. He wouldn't put an elaborate inscription on them, but he would say, "To so and so with best wishes." Sometimes he'd just sign his name and give it to the child.

Q: You have a cute picture here taken of Sunnyvale, California - where he's in the middle of a bunch of children that I want to take.

Mr. C.: All right. That was a dedication of a school, an elementary school, the Chester W. Nimitz School, one of several.

Q: Now, let's see, what dates are we talking about? First, you were with him in '46 and '47 in Washington, then you stayed on for a year in 1948 in Washington with Admiral Denfeld?

Mr. C.: Yes, and then, I think it was '49, that I ...

Q: That you came here?

Mr. C.: ... came out to California

Q: And this was because Admiral Nimitz requested you?

Mr. C.: Yes.

Q: And then you stayed with them through the rest of your career?

Mr. C.: Through the rest of my career.

Q: Which was how many years?

Mr. C.: Well, I retired in 1961.

Q: That would have been eleven more years, which means you were with him 14 years, so you must have known him as closely as any male

Mr. C.: I would say yes, definitely. But it's hard to go back and recount things ...

Q: I'm going to ask you some individual questions in a minute, but I wanted to note the chronological story. I didn't want to interrupt the chronological story. You've told me what your activities, and what his activities, were pretty much in San

Francisco, and this was from '49 until ... When did he go back to the United Nations?

Mr. C.: I think that was probably in early '49, I can't remember now.

Q: You have a letter from him in February of '50 from the United Nations ...

Mr. C.: It was probably early '49.

Q: And did you go back with him?

Mr. C.: I went back to the United Nations with him.

Q: And what was his attitude there? And his feelings about that job?

Mr. C.: At first he was pretty much enthused. In later life, I think he really hated to leave this area because he loved it. He loved San Francisco, and he loved Berkeley and the hills. At that time he was pretty much enthused, and I think that when he got back to the UN he figured that the plebiscite mission would be formed, and we'd be off in just a month or so time. But it drug out and the issue still hasn't been settled today. It drug out over a long period of time and, of course, his enthusiasm waned, and I believe he thought that the nations concerned would somehow come to an early agreement, like people used to do in the service.

You meet only for so long and you settle for some sort of agreement, but the UN doesn't operate that way, and to get hundreds of people to agree on the same thing in a short time was impossible

Q: How long did he stay in the East?

Mr. C.: Oh, he must have stayed there — again, my memory fails — for many months.

Q: Did he feel he accomplished anything on it?

Mr. C.: I believe so. He was quite sensational around the United Nations. He was quite different than anyone that they had been used to. He was already a celebrity in his own right, and he was a beautiful man, physically a beautiful person with that snow-white hair and blue eyes.

Q: Did he wear uniform then?

Mr. C.: He wore civilian clothes for the most part, and his uniform occasionally. His manner made his stand out — he had an air about him.

Q: Air of authority?

Mr. C.: Not authority, really, but this is something that made him stand out ...

Q: A manner of distinction is the way they say in ...

Mr. C.: Yet a man that you could approach, a man who smiled easily was friendly, and kind, and considerate. He was something quite unusual.

Q: Did he do any incident there that indicated to you his concern in details of people's lives - I'm thinking of the swimming incident.

Mr. C.: When he first went to the United Nations he thought he was just going to be there a short while, and he was living in a hotel in downtown Manhattan. I was over at Brooklyn in a YMCA. I would meet him in the morning - we were using a Navy car. I kept the car at the Brooklyn Navy Yard since I was living in Brooklyn. I'd meet him in the morning, and we'd go to the UN at Lake Success. Finally, after a period of time it was obvious that he was going to be around for a while. He had some friends out on Long Island, and he moved out to Oyster Bay, and stayed there. We could go swimming in the Long Island Sound. The Admiral the first evenings we were there would jump in and take a swim. The wife of the couple we were staying with was very concerned because with the Admiral swimming around out there she figured something might happen, and she told me to play lifeguard one evening. I said, "If I swim out as far as the Admiral is right now I may be in trouble, and you'll have to rescue me, because I can't swim as well as he can." So when he came back in she told him that maybe I should go swimming at the same time he did. He said, "Why don't you go swimming?" I said, "Well, I don't have a bathing suit." So he said, "Well, you can borrow one of mine tomorrow," and I said, "Fine." The next morning we were going to the UN, through this small town, and he said, "Pull up in front of this drug store for a minute." He went in, came back out, got in the car, and as we drove down the street he said, "Here, this is for you. You'll need it with my bathing trunks." It was an athletic supporter that he'd bought me to wear.

Q: The detail that he could think of is astonishing, isn't it?

Mr. C.: Yes, with all the other things he had on his mind. He thought that he should have a complete swimming costume for me.

There were a lot of things that took place when he was Chief of Naval Operations, things that I remember as we go along. He was very much concerned with my welfare. He had a lot more patience with me than I would have had for any young man at the time. I'd been in the Marine Corps for a while, and Marine Corps outfits were a good bit more rough and tough, and there was not much refinement. This was the way life was lived, and here I was being exposed to a gentleman. Some of the things I did must have been a trial for him. The Admiral was a man who appreciated fine music. He went to the symphony, he loved opera. The first couple of times he tried to expose me to a symphony I sort of rebeled - I didn't take too kindly to it. I don't think I'd have had the patience that he had. I believe the first time he gave me tickets I said, "No," or something like that. Slowly he brought me around to the point where I started to acquire a little liking for it. People would give him books - hundreds of books arrived at his office as gifts, including first editions. He couldn't read all of them. He read a lot, constantly as a matter of fact. He gave me many books to read, and I would give him a very short book review.

Thanks to him I read a lot more and a greater variety than I would have ordinarily at that stage of my life.

Q: Do you know what his favorite symphony was?

Mr. C.: No.

Q: Or his favorite author?

Mr. C.: No. He admired the writing of Samuel Eliot Morison, but I can't say he was his favorite. He was very much interested in history and historical events, particularly, of course, anything to do with the Navy and sea power.

Q: Do you know what his favorite food was?

Mr. C.: No. Mrs. Nimitz would have to fill you in on that. He believed in simplicity in the kitchen. On days when Mrs. Nimitz would be out Admiral Nimitz and I would fix a lunch together.

Q: This is after you came to Berkeley?

Mr. C.: Right. He had his own idea of how a couple of gentlemen fixed a lunch. After all, women always spend a lot more time in the kitchen than is necessary, and this whole operation could be a lot more efficient. We didn't need all those pots and pans, maybe we could make ourselves a bowl of soup because that would only take one pan and a couple of bowls. We could, maybe, tear up a little lettuce for a salad, and really there was no use going to a great amount of fuss. Some of the things that we concocted were spectacular. Of course there was always bread, which was easy. And by using a very, very small amount of kitchen equipment we were being efficient. He'd say, "Wasn't that a delicious meal? We had salad and soup (and whatever else we could make simply), and we won't take hours to clean up. Here, you wash those dishes and I'll clean up these pots." He would souse water around like crazy, hang a pot on the wall, and water would be running down the wall. The sink was kind of a mess, but it was a very efficient operation. I always wondered what his wife would think of the kitchen when she returned, because it was very efficient. We were very quick and there was no fooling around when two men had their lunch. He was very interesting that way.

He also had an idea when he was Chief of Naval Operations - that was the time he discovered electric razors ...

He discovered electric razors and he thought that they were the only way to shave. He sort of insisted that I use one also, and that in time my whiskers would get accustomed to this shaving technique. In fact he took one of his razors and autographed it to me. I happened to grab it out of the drawer the other night, and I think it's probably the only autographed electric razor in the country.

Q: It probably is.

Mr. C.: And I put a piece of paper over the autograph to try to protect it ...

Cozard - 33

Q: And it has his initials on it in silver - CWN, USN. It looks brand new ...

Mr. C.: Oh, I've used it several times. I took it to Remington and they repaired it without a charge. I never could use the razor, but I thought it was a beautiful thing to have. I don't think that there's another one around like that.

Q: When you speak of that, I think you ought to speak of this very nice glass from which I'm drinking. It's inscribed with the initials of CWN on it.

Mr. C.: Well, you see, he was very much concerned about my nutrition and well being. Mrs. Nimitz was too. They were both very good about looking after me.

Q: Because you were a bachelor?

Mr. C.: Yes. When I first met the Admiral I was single, and in 1947 I was married. The wedding was at the Naval Air Station, the Anacostia Naval Air Station. Admiral and Mrs. Nimitz were there. We had side boys, and a naval chaplain, a Marine buddy of mine was best man. Up until that time I was living with an old retired Marine and his wife in Southeast Washington. We had a reception at the old Marine's house. It was a beautiful affair. We were married for about ten years or so, and then, as things happen we were divorced. I was single for about a year, then I met a girl, maybe through force of habit or something, but she was a beautiful girl, and I loved her and her family, and we were married. And it was obvious right from the start that it wasn't going to work out. Mrs. Nimitz told me much later that the Admiral was very much concerned. He wasn't happy about the whole affair.

Q: He didn't give you any advice at the time?

Mr. C.: Oh, no, none. But he had told Mrs. Nimitz that he was very unhappy with the idea. I was smitten and I didn't see anything but what I wanted to see. I stayed married for just a short while and was divorced. Ever since then I've been living alone, and in between marriages I was living alone. He was concerned that I should have proper utensils. They always asked me if I had a nice place, and they came to the several different places I lived many times. He was concerned that I had a place to fix breakfast, and look after myself. The Admiral decided that I should have some of his glasses — the little glas that you have there with his name on it — so that in the morning I could drink my fruit juice. I looked around the apartment the other day and discovered it. He gave me the glasses because that way, at least, I would remember to drink juice in the morning and my nutritional needs would be taken care of.

Q: I think the story of the scarf he gave you is nice, too.

Mr. C.: After he left the active duty part of his life we wore civilian clothes quite a bit of the time, for if Admiral Nimitz walked down Main Street in uniform we certainly weren't going to keep our time schedule. He was kind enough to visit with everyone and give them a bit of his time - the Admiral in uniform was spectacular - and progress was always very slow. So we wore civilian clothes. I was always used to being out in the open; I didn't wear a hat and I didn't wear a scarf, and he was very concerned that I would catch cold. So, one day he went out and got a scarf and presented me with it.

Q: He not only gave you advice, he did the things to make you do it.

Mr. C.: One time we were out somewhere and he said, "Do you have a handkerchief?" I said, "No." He gave me a handkerchief to put in my breast pocket. I happened to find it the other day.

Q: It has his initials on it?

Mr. C.: Yes. I was surprised going through the house at how many bits and pieces that I found in every room that had something to do with Admiral Nimitz. I thought that after moving around over the years, living in many places, and now pursuing a different line of work, that there were very few Nimitz things around. I started to look around and in every room I found something - books autographed, pictures. Once he gave me a little book on how to avoid financial tangles, how to invest your money properly. I found the razor, drinking glasses, scarves, and I found this little thing here. Many times I took Admiral Nimitz over to the White House; one time he swiped this little matchbook from Mr. Truman's office and autographed it with the date.

Q: Was he susceptible to colds? Was he worried about catching cold?

Mr. C.: I think that was the only really weak spot in his physical makeup, maybe not the only one. His back bothered him from time to time. When the Admiral got a cold it wasn't like the ordinary cold that I'd catch. A cold really floored him, and it would take him a matter of days - several times he was in the hospital. I know in the East at least once, and in England on one occasion he spent several days in the hospital. Colds really knocked him for a loop.

Q: Did he ever have pneumonia that you know of?

Mr. C.: Yes, I believe he did.

Q: But he did have a susceptibility, then?

Mr. C.: Oh, definitely. He had a couple of hernia operations. His last operation was over at Oak Knoll Hospital, and, of course, I went over to visit with him every day, and he showed me his incision. I remember after he'd been in the hospital for the last hernia operation - he'd been in the hospital about four days - he pulled back the coverlet and showed me his incision and he said, "I think I'll be ready to go home in about another day, don't you?" I said, "Yes sir," so he said, "Well, tell the doctor." He'd made up his mind he was going to be discharged from the hospital, he was like that you know.

Of course, he's buried in Golden Gate Cemetery in San Bruno. We went out there to pick out a spot many years before his death. He wanted to have a place where some of his old companions from the Pacific could be buried along with their wives, and eventually a place for his wife. We picked out a section there. Admiral Spruance was buried out there just a short while back - I went to his funeral about three weeks back ...

Q: Within the last month.

Mr. C.: Also Admiral Turner. Many years ago Admiral Nimitz drew up burial plans well in advance. His burial plans were drawn up in, oh, about 1949, or somewhere near that time - way back.

Q: Did he feel - was he depressed about it or

Mr. C.: Yes, he said he didn't want to go back until his time came. The Admiral was, I think, very fearful of dying. He was a very strong man, and he couldn't stand the thought of being an invalid, or of having a lingering illness. I think he was very much afraid of dying.

Q: Did he ever discuss his philosophy of life or death or ...? Was he a religious man?

Mr. C.: Not as such. He wasn't a churchgoer.

Q: His daughter became a nun.

Mr. C.: His youngest daughter is a Dominican nun.

Q: Did you ever hear him comment about that?

Mr. C.: Oh, he was very pleased. She's in a teaching order, and she's doing something very, very helpful for humanity.

Q: And he was pleased with that?

Mr. C.: It pleased him. I think that most of the children were educated in Catholic high schools.

I was going to tell you — when we picked this spot out for his burial, he worked out his own plan, and he put down the names of the people he wanted to be honorary pallbearers, and those to be in attendance, and those in charge of the arrangements, and, of course, most all the ones he had picked on to be pallbearers ...

Q: Predeceased him?

Mr. C.: Yes, that's right, or were infirm.

I asked him a couple of times, I said, "Listen, Admiral I'm very concerned about where I'm going to end up, and I'd certainly like to have a spot out there in the cemetery somewhere near you."

And he said, "Well, the only way that I can guarantee you that is to go a couple of minutes before I do." It never came to pass. I thought that was a very nice answer for him to give, though.

Q: I was going to ask you - you said that you knew him at the time he was writing Sea Power, or at least editing it with Mr. Potter, who is the biographer for Admiral Nimitz. Do you recall any incidents relating to that?

Mr. C.: No, not right now. I'd have to go through it and read it again. I can't recall anything about that at the moment.

I can recall when the Admiral was technical advisor for the movie "John Paul Jones." I think he was a little confused by some of the people in Hollywood. He wanted things to be done according to history. He wanted the leading man to look like John Paul Jones, not like leading men look according to Hollywood standards. He really was concerned with the facts, the historical facts being correct.

He was a man who had great patience - he had great patience with me - and we spent quite a bit of time together either walking or in his study or when he was working. I would take his mail to his house. Sometimes he took great pride in telling people, "Look, here's an invitation, or here's a letter, and here's the answer to go with it," because I knew how he would respond, and I could anticipate him, and he'd receive his invitation or his letter along with the answer. I knew exactly what he was going to do, and so I would have the answer typed, and present it to him for his signature. He thought I was extremely ...

Q: Of course, that's the finest of staff work.

Mr. C.: And when two people know each other -- he was really more like family to me, perhaps more than my own family because I left home when I was a young man.

Q: How old were you when you started working for Admiral Nimitz?

Mr. C.: Well, let's see. I must have been possibly 24, maybe 25 years old. I don't remember.

Q: So your growing up time practically was with him.

Mr. C.: Oh, yes, and I think I was a very late bloomer, a slow developer. I was steady, which was great. I guess he saw potential that I didn't see. In later years, he made sure that I had time to go to school at nights, and was interested in furthering my education and my advancing. He told me many times when I retired from the Marine Corps and went to work at P.G.and E. - "Before I die I hope to see you as president of the company." That was nice to hear, but quite impossible.

Q: No, but it showed his faith in you.

Mr. C.: It was his way of showing faith in me.

Q: I'm sure he's been a motivating factor -- I shouldn't speak for you, but I would guess he was the motivating factor in your life.

Mr. C.: He was, our relationship completely changed the course of my life. I have no idea where I would have gone if I hadn't met him. It wasn't until many years later -after I retired - I talked to him on the telephone every couple of days, I'd call him and talk to him. We talked about my job, the news, and people we knew. I knew his friends, and the order things fell into. We could talk easily like two people with knowledge about the same subject, our conversations were very candid. The little notes he sent me and letters in his handwriting were very candid.

Q: He thought toward you probably like a son.

Mr. C.: Yes, I think he did.

Q: Do you remember any of his stories, or witticisms? How did he greet you?

Mr. C.: He called me by my last name.

Q: Yes, I would expect that.

Mr. C.: And I called him "Admiral." That is the way it always was.

Q: Always, and through all of your relationships?

Mr. C.: There was such a great rank spread between us - a Fleet Admiral and a master sergeant. Yet, we still had a personal friendship, still we observed certain traditional rules of the service.

Cozard - 42

Q: You set your own rules, I'm sure -- again I'm speaking for you, but I'm sure the fact that you played your own rules is what made you invaluable to him.

Mr. C.: Possibly so. A couple of times I said, "Admiral I know that other people who had worked around officers and cabinet members have used ranking persons names in saying - I want this and I want that, it's very damaging to a man's reputation," and I said, "I've never really asked for anything for myself using your name. I never will. You're the Admiral, and I'm the master sergeant. As far as I'm concerned that's the way it is, and we get things on the up and up that you want, but not things for me."

Q: But to go back to the stories, can you remember any of the stories that he told? Or did you ever hear him tell any stories?

Mr. C.: I can remember one time when he hid his sword under the bed - I don't know whether I should tell this or not...

Q: Of course you should.

Mr. C.: But he disliked wearing a sword, you know going to affairs where you had to wear a sword. He slid his sword under the bed and said, "If I can't find it I won't have to wear it." He didn't wear his sword at all after that. He had lots of stories that he recounted about the early days, and his early times, and things that happened ...

Q: I understood, though, he was a story teller ...

Cozard - 43

Mr. C.: Oh, a great story teller.

Q: Well, that's what I wondered. Can you remember any of his stories?

Mr. C.: I probably can later on.

Q: In the middle of the night?

Mr. C.: In the middle of the night, possibly.

I started to tell you a minute ago about his seeing that I got schooled and aimed in the right direction. As I have come along and learned things over the years there have been many times when I would say to myself, "Admiral, I know now what you were trying to tell me then."

He was a man with great insight. And when we first started to use rocketry in warfare he was very much concerned, he was very much concerned with indiscriminate bombing. He thought that warfare should be confined to the military rather than hurting innocent people.

Q: Oh, you met him, of course, after Hiroshima. I wondered if you ever heard him express his opinion about the dropping of the atomic bomb?

Mr. C.: Maybe he did over the years, but now it has slipped my mind.

Q: But this will come back to you in rough form, and in the meantime I would love you to make notes of things that you remember in the quiet hours of the night or even after I leave -

you'll probably say why didn't I think of that. So make a note and add it to the manuscript, and then it will come back in a smooth copy ...

Mr. C.: Oh, there'll be many things that come back. I'm sure that there were so many things that happened in the 1946-47 period that I'll recall. Of course the things later in life stick in my mind.

The Admiral got to checking on massagers. He took a liking to cyclo-massage devices, and he had a couple of them. He had one in his bathroom right off his downstairs study. A couple of times during that period I'd show up at his house rather early to take him to some function or for some other purpose, and he would say, "Now, why don't you just get off your clothes and get in the bathtub there, and turn on the massage - it will really ease the pains in your back." I jumped in one time I was there, let the water run for a while and got in the tub for a few minutes, and came out and started to get dressed, and he said, "I'm not ready yet. Why don't you get back in, you haven't been in long enough at all." I think I got out of there once or twice with my fingers and toes wrinkled as prunes. He believed in sunbathing in the nude. He had a place down behind his garden house, and I don't know if his wife was terrified or not that someone would catch him, but he frequently went sunbathing in the nude behind the garden house.

I told you he was a great horse shoe pitcher, and he loved pitching horse shoes in an area that he prepared himself. He was just fantastic and now and then when we played at a time such as that we'd take little cuts at each other, and I'd tease him about his pitching.

Q: Do you remember his philosophy that he would tell you about how you should guide your life, or maybe do it more by just saying go to school or some such thing?

Mr. C.: Well, he sort of aimed me by stressing educational aspects, also guiding me using other people as examples. Later on, when I retired, there were two other Marines who served with him during the final years. Also there was an aide assigned to him, a Commander I believe, The Public Information Office, or Public Affairs Office, did a lot of his work for him. He used to use me as an example for the other Marines to follow. According to them he'd often say, "Now, look what he did. That's the way you should go about it." I thought that was really great.

Q: Who did he cite as an example you should follow, do you recall?

Mr. C.: Of course, his son was one. He retired and took a job in industry - that was one of my guides. He also mentioned several times remarks different people in industries had made about me, and thought these might be good ideas to consider.

Q: Then he was always thinking of you?

Mr. C.: Oh, definitely. He was just a sweetheart. Quite often now I keep wishing, "Oh, God, I wish you were back so that I could tell you that. I see now what you were trying to tell me. I appreciate your guidance and patience. How great it really was."

Q: I think people many times - probably all of us feel that way about our parents - if only I could tell you now that I know what you meant, and how I appreciate what you did for me, but never probably said the words and, in effect, you're just saying that you felt like he was your father.

Mr. C.: Yes.

Q: Is that being too sentimental?

Mr. C.: No, I don't think so.

Q: I don't either. He was quoted as saying to a friend of mine who made some statement that was sentimental, and he said, "Sentiment is a great part of a naval officers career - life."

Mr. C.: He loved the soil. He loved gardening.

Q: And animals and children. And all of this, and yet he was able to fight and win a war. Isn't it incredible?

Mr. C.: It is.

Q: Well, you've given some personal detail that I'm sure nobody else would know, except maybe his wife, and sometimes people that are that close maybe don't see the characteristics that someone such as yourself does.

Mr. C.: That's true. I was sort of hoping I wouldn't inject too much of me in there, but it's the only way I feel ...

Q: I don't see how you could help it.

Mr. C.: But there were so many things that were just part of our lives, the things that we did together just won't stay out of my mind - day to day routine things. And we were just sort of living around each other and living together. I had his complete trust - I really valued that. When he left to go off on a trip he lent me his house, his car - he often wrote back and asked if I was enjoying the patio and the sunshine.

When I first started working with him back in 1946, we were going down to the office one day and he asked me how I felt about something. I said, "Do you want the truth?" and he said, "Yes." And I told him straight - I think that's the way our relationship evolved. It was just an honest, open thing all the way through, and it got to the point where we just became a team.

I grabbed up some old copies - I had them out for some reason - of fitness reports to show you some of the language that he used. He started stressing in my fitness reports later my way of applying myself, the things I had done ..

Q: He never hesitated to say a nice word about people ...

Mr. C.: No, never.

We talked one time about something when he was ill and he said, "Thank you," and I said, "There is no reason to thank me."

Quite often he'd thank me for things; Mrs. Nimitz would thank me for things. They would thank me in front of other people, which was very nice. There was no reason to thank me, you know, there really isn't. I think that if you ever need anything, even blood, it's not a question of how much, it's just a question of the sleeve you want rolled up.

I wore some of his clothes, you know, things that were of a personal nature. And it was - you couldn't say it was a father and son relationship - it was a friendship between two men, our relationship. I think we had a great deal of respect for each other.

Q: Oh, I'm sure.

Mr. C.: I could drive the car well. He wasn't very good as a navigator of a car.

Q: Was he a good driver?

Mr. C.: No, no, he wasn't. He was really something behind the whe

Q: He hadn't very much occasion to drive, though, had he?

Mr. C.: No, he hadn't, other people had taken care of those chores for him. When he got behind the wheel he went along okay, but he sort of navigated the car, rather than driving it. If he went around one particular corner, and he swept a little wide, and maybe bounced off a pole just enough to scratch or bend a fender, later o he'd say, "Let's not go that way. I think this street over here's a better street." And he would kind of avoid any spot where he had a little bash with some immovable subject. And I think that's where we had some respect. I could drive the car fine, he couldn't, but he did other things, but I could repair the cigarette lighter. He could beat me at horse shoes, and this was really great, I mean sort of blended in together. I'd get a tickle out of finding that someone who's that great, has that much ability, is human after all.

Q: I think it's interesting that the little mechanical things he let somebody else do.

Mr. C.: He learned to repair quite a few mechanical things later in life when he had more time for tinkering.

So he started writing - the Admiral really was concerned about getting me a commission before I retired. He was very much concerned with that. He wanted me to be able to use the officers' clubs and things of this nature. I was very happy being a master sergeant, because that was a nice role to play, and I enjoyed it. I never felt that that was such a bad spot to be in, but I was tickled by the idea. I would have liked to have been commissioned, and he really stressed in several of his fitness reports and letters to different people that he would like to have me commissioned.

Q: At this point in history it seems kind of unimportant, though, doesn't it?

Mr. C.: It really didn't matter.

Q: Oh, with him, probably. But had you become a commissioned officer then you would have had a different ...

Mr. C.: Entirely different life.

Q: Other aspects of your career would have opened up.

Mr. C.: Entirely different. This way I could be the brash upstart youngster he helped form.

Several spots here are underlined in some of his letters and fitness reports. Here's a letter from Admiral to General Shoup - just a few parts here underlined are interesting.

Q: Yes. He says you're the sole member of his personal staff and acts as aide, administers the office, reads his mail, and you took the place of a personal staff provided for officers of his rank on active duty. That's a wonderful tribute, isn't it?

Mr. C.: Here's a few more excerpts. Note the type of language he uses. He does all this, you notice, in longhand.

Q: Yes. I think that's interesting. Wonderful compliment.

Mr. C.: Then you'll notice as I started to head toward the public relations field ...

Q: He stresses that, I expect.

Mr. C.: Yes.

Q: Yes. "First he assists in the maintenance of my public relations which, after all, is the principal reason for my being kept on the active list, and attends night classes in public relations."

Mr. C.: He was very proud of that.

Q: He's quite shrewd, isn't he?

Mr. C.: Sure, and he stresses this in about three of four fitness reports.

Q: "Particularly well qualified to duty in public relations."

Mr. C.: Then, you see how well his minds works. Here is ...

Q: "Tactful to a high degree and particularly successful in dealing with the many (what's this?) civilians with whom I have contact."

Mr. C.: Yes. See this part, right here, the first line. I don't know if you can make out his writing. I can make out everything that he wrote over the years.

Q: "Performed most satisfactorily his duties as the sole assistant to me in my capacity as special assistant to the Secretary of the Navy." He says it's a special duty.

Mr. C.: He was very proud of the fact that he only had one person serving with him, and he wasn't tying up many naval personnel, and that he was keeping costs down. That's the reason, I'm sure, a lot of times he stressed that I was the sole member of his staff - this showed he only had one person and he was utilizing me effectively.

When he went out of town a lot of time he would have me work for other people to make sure that my time was used. I worked for the Commandant of the 12th Naval District, for the Commander of the Western Sea Frontier, and I was sent off on different duties. I mentioned one time I went down to the Naval Line School. And one time when the Shah of Iran first visited the U. S. and appeared to be shopping around for a wife or some such thing, I went to the airport to pick up the Shah of Iran, and drove him during his stay in San Francisco - I don't know how I got involved in it exactly. And quite often I'd get mixed up in driving and escorting high ranking people.

Q: Now, when did you retire?

Mr. C.: 1961

Q: 1961, and that was when you left Admiral Nimitz, of course?

Mr. C.: Yes.

Q: Well, I think the things you've said are stories, again, that nobody else would know, and I'm sure you fleshed out some of the bones of his character and his activities, especially in this period when he left the Pacific, but still you talk about his characteristics which were always there.

Mr. C.: I was trying to give you the personal, the human side of Admiral Nimitz, because he was human and ...

Q: Mrs. Nimitz did recommend that we talk to you, as you probably know.

Mr. C.: I think I read that in one of the letters.

When the Admiral was Chief of Naval Operations that was my first contact with him, and, as I said, I serviced his needs for transportation, or I carried messages for him quite often, and so was thoroughly exposed to all the things he was doing. I know I overheard conversations, I knew where he was going and for what reason, I went with him or somehow got involved in it, and I enjoyed every minute of it. These were all of his official duties, and a lot of his social duties, and I, perhaps, was dwelling more on the things that happened later in life. There were a lot of things that went on then that I can't quite bring back.

I went with him one time to Winchester, Virginia, to the Apple Blossom Festival, and we went to Senator Byrd's home and I met Admiral Byrd. When Admiral Byrd went back to the Antarctic, that would be about '46 or '47, I really wanted to go. I thought it would be a great adventure. I was young enough - the Admiral kind of talked me out of that. I thought that would be a great adventure to go on.

And, of course, there are just so many different things that happened, and so many meetings - late meetings - at night having to do with the Navy. And, of course, the Navy was being cut down considerably in size at that time. I can remember when Mr. Forrestal was Secretary of the Navy, before he became Secretary of Defense, taking him to Forrestal's house, waiting many hours.

Q: Try to remember, if you can, the things between now and when you get the manuscript back, which I hope won't be too long, and feel free to add them to it.

Mr. C.: Will I be seeing you again, or ...?

Q: No, not necessarily, because this will be sent to you directly. Unless you decide you have enough to put on another tape, and then tell Mr. Mason and ...

Mr. C.: I don't believe I'd have enough. If I really had things - questions - I need people who were around at that time - I possibly could come up with little bits and pieces of things that happened. It's too bad that so many years went by. All the Admiral's files of course were sent back to ...

Q: I think his son has them. He would never write a book.

Mr. C.: No, he didn't want that. He always said that possibly his children would write it.

Q; But I understand they don't want to either, and so I'm awfully glad it isn't being delayed any longer, and I think because Mr. Pott worked with him he's a marvellous choice.

Mr. C.: He is. It shouldn't be delayed.

In the San Francisco area we have several things named in honor of Admiral Nimitz. There's a Nimitz and MacArthur Street, both in the same little tract. I found them one day and told the Admiral. Later he took some of his guests on a cruise around those little streets.

Of course there is the Nimitz Freeway which runs from Oakland to San Jose. Having it named for him always bothered the Admiral. He handed me the paper one day and said, "The headlines say two killed on Nimitz." He hated to see this type of thing. When he mentioned the Freeway, which was quite often, I used to say, "Yes, Admiral, but think of the large volume of traffic it carries. Accidents are bound to happen."

The story of Admiral Nimitz should not be delayed. Many times when I have had children with me, and have been driving on the Freeway I have told them - "This is the Nimitz Freeway, you know it's named for Admiral Nimitz." Most of them have no idea who Admiral Nimitz was. We live in an entirely different world now, and this part of history should not go unrecorded.

Q: Well, that's wonderful. I'm just awfully glad that they're writing it now, even though it's considerably delayed.

Mr. C.: He was an absolutely amazing man. He was a kind, considerate, intelligent, he was just an all-around beautiful person. Even when he lost his temper - sometimes he couldn't quite understand why products had to become obsolete, or why an item that could be made for 15 cents couldn't be sold for that. I had a hard time explaining to him that everybody had to make a living and ...

Q: Why, yes. After all, he did live almost by a socialistic system - a dirty word. But he would not have understood that either, I shouldn't think.

Well, I've just loved the day, and I thank you for your hospitality and for the pictures, and I'll send them back and they will be returned to you.

Mr. C.: Well, thank you very much. I hope I've been something of a help.

Q: Oh, wonderful. It surely has been fine.

Interview # 2

George Cozard by Etta Belle Kitchen
April 21, 1970

Subject: Admiral Nimitz

Miss Kitchen: Mr. Mason, this is an addendum to the previous George Cozard interview about Admiral Nimitz. He gave this to me in shorthand when I didn't have my recorder. So I am going to put in on tape for your information and use if you wish. The following are quotations.

Mr. Cozard: When you were in San Francisco we mentioned that perhaps later on things would come back to me concerning the life of Admiral Nimitz.

The official records of the war will show that he was a great military leader. We have a way of cleaning up history to the point where everything comes off on schedule and every battle is executed flawlessly. I want to give you more of the human side of Admiral Nimitz.

He certainly was not a person without flaws. It is fortunate for us that he happened to be the right person selected for the job at the right time. He was not perfect, but I have never in my time in the service met another Admiral who had the all around abilities and combination of abilities that he had.

You asked what his comments were when he arrived at Pearl Harbor. This has probably been recorded elsewhere, but I happened to think of some of the comments he made over the years.

He always stated that the Japanese made a mistake in attacking the ships in the harbor. They should have destroyed the above ground fuel storage areas. This would have crippled the fleet.

He also said had there been a second attack, he believed the island could have been invaded successfully.

He said it was a blessing that Admiral Kimmel had not been warned, because if he had sent the fleet to sea it might have been destroyed. Fortunately the ships were located in the harbor at a place where they could be salvaged and repaired.

He also spoke many times of the value of the weather reports — Japanese weather reports - which were intercepted. Because prevailing winds come from the west to east, and the weather the Japanese were experiencing one day the fleet would experience the next day. The Navy could thus prepare and conduct it's operations based on weather reports which were vital to their operation.

Later in his life he spent quite a bit of time studying the weather. He had a rain gauge in his yard, and a submarine model weathervane on his garden house. He paid close attention to the wind direction and velocity.

He also had a large pair of Japanese binoculars mounted on a tripod in his yard.

He mentioned several times that part of our success was due to our having radar. The Japanese were limited to the use of binoculars, which limited their observations to the line of sight.

During his later years in Berkeley, his mind was still very active, and he was still concerned with everything that happened in the area. He quite often remarked about the lack of shipping in our large San Francisco harbor. He said trade with China would certainly be beneficial, and he thought it would fill our port with ships. He thought the exchange of goods would be beneficial to both nations. He sighed the fact that the Japanese and the Chinese were trading.

He quite often made predictions which were quite amazing. Several times in the early 1950s he said the east side of San Francisco Bay would at some future date be filled in from the area around Berkeley to the Bay Bridge. He said the land would be very valuable for industrial purposes. And that is being done at this time. Quite a few new restaurants and other facilities are being built and planned in that area now.

One day when we were driving through the San Ramon area, east of Oakland, which was at that time open farm land, he suggested someone with enough foresight to buy land in that area would be in a good financial position in the future. The area is now being developed. Several new large towns have sprung up and there are several industrial parks in the process of being developed.

The Admiral had a very strong sense of history. He spent quite a bit of time studying the past and contemplating the future.

He was a confirmed Navy man. He was convinced that we would always need ships, that a large merchant fleet was vital to our nation.

This story was a favorite of his, and he repeated it many times until his death. The story goes like this:

From an open letter to junior officers from Fleet Admiral Chester Nimitz, USN, published in the February 1960 issue of the United States Naval Institute PROCEEDINGS.

"On 7 September '56 I was invited to attend an official reception in San Francisco. Enroute to the reception I mentioned to master sergeant George E. Cozard, USMC, an old friend of many years, that this date 7 September had a special meaning for me. It marked the anniversary of my entrance to the United States Naval Academy and the Navy 55 years earlier. After a moment's thought Cozard asked, "Admiral, do you intend to make a career of the Navy?" To which I replied in a hearty affirmative. You may be sure I sincerely meant just that, and I still do."

Miss Kitchen: I think it's repeated in SHIPMATE, and also in the Institute in one of the issues.

Cozard: I mentioned the first time we talked that Admiral Nimitz was somewhat baffled by small mechanical objects. Later when he was living in Berkeley, and had more time, he developed a little more skill in dealing with repairs.

He bought a zipper repair kit and became the neighborhood zipper repair expert.

He became quite fascinated with knife sharpening. I even took him some of my knives at his request. He got so carried away with sharpening them that about half of one of my knives was gone before he stopped.

He was quite pleased with his new-found skills. He enjoyed trips to the hardware stores and became close friends with the people in the stores.

His daytime dress was very informal, usually an old pair of shorts or an old t-shirt, and a pair of boondockers (field boots). He would go downtown shopping in this costume. But he was still Admiral Nimitz, and recognized no matter what he wore. For the most part his attire was very rustic.

He was a very humble man. He was not a stereotype military figure. I'm sure people reading the factial accounts of the second World War would have no conception of Admiral Nimitz. He was not without flaws, but he was a unique personality.

Of the many medals he was awarded he only wore two, quite unlike the pictures of the great military men of that period with chests covered with ribbons and worn with a certain amount of flamboyance.

The two medals which Admiral Nimitz wore and prized were the Distinguished Service Medal and a silver Life Saving Medal. Later some time after his term as CNO had expired he added one more ribbon. I can't remember which one it was.

He only wore one row of ribbons. He did not care for show. He was bothered by wearing a sword on ceremonial occasions. It was against his nature to put on a big display with sword and medals.

He was also a very proud man. He was proud of keeping his weight to almost the same as it was in his Naval Academy days.

I have not mentioned one big flaw in Admiral Nimitz, and it may be hard to pick one out. Simply because his greatest asset was his ability to put people at ease and smooth out differences. Perhaps this is why it is hard to find a flaw, because there never was a jarring note when he was around.

When I talked of my relationships with him earlier I mentioned the fact that perhaps he was a father figure. I believe we had a mutual admiration society and a great deal of respect for each other. When two men feel that way it is a wonderful thing. Service men quite often have a close feeling through shared experiences, and it is a strong type of affection, stronger perhaps than some husbands and wives have.

The Admiral certainly was not without physical ailments. I had quite a bit of correspondence from him, all in long hand and over a long period of years, starting from the early fifties through the rest of his life.

He repeatedly refers to having colds which he says hit him 'like a bolt' or 'floored him.' He was in and out of the hospital many times due to respiratory problems. He mentions quite often having trouble with his back.

He was really a beautiful person. He was a beautiful person quite a few years before the flower generation helped us to become aware of beauty of the spirit as well as physical beauty. The people in Berkeley and the Bay area loved to see him, and constantly stopped to talk to him.

I was searching my comments trying to find words to describe him, but all I can think is that he had 'charisma' long before the word became popular. Certainly people who have been referred to as having charisma are human, but yet the air about them dismisses any frailties and flaws. His charm overrode any possible flaws. He was not a saint. He knew his share of off-color stories.

Miss Kitchen: I asked him if he couldn't remember any of Admiral Nimitz's stories, and finally Mr. Cozard came up with this one.

Mr. Cozard: One simple story is about the Marines who landed on an island and noticed a dead animal lying on the beach. After a couple of days it started to smell. The company officer sent some Marines to bury it. One of them said, "It's a dead mule." Another one said, "No, it's too small to be a mule, it's a donkey." They asked a Chaplain to settle the issue. He said, "According to the scriptures that is an ass." They continued digging. A group of Marines on their way back from the front lines yelled over, "Hey, what are you guys digging, a fox hole?" One of them replied, "No, not according to the scriptures."

He was full of life, he enjoyed life, he had a twinkle in his eye. It was a blessing that he died when he did. He had several strokes and would have been an invalid and the charisma would have gone, and he would not have been the Admiral Nimitz that we all knew and loved. He lived a full life, and I'm sure he enjoyed it. We are all fortunate for having had him and the opportunity to know him, for his type will never pass this way again.

Miss Kitchen: A few footnotes:

Mr. Cozard said that a book was written entitled ABANDON SHIP about the sinking of the INDIANAPOLIS. The parents of one of the boys lost on that ship sent the book to Admiral Nimitz with certain parts underlined, and a letter which accused him of being responsible in part for the loss of the ship and their boy's life.

Admiral Nimitz's response was one of shock and dismay. He was almost, on one of the rare occasions, at a loss as to what to say or how to react.

Mr. Cozard was not sure whether he replied to it or not. Many times he had George draft the reply, but in this case he simply took the letter and it wasn't mentioned again. But he wasn't enthusiastic about replying, and if he did reply George never saw it.

Another note: Admiral Nimitz refused many job offers from industry. He said his allegiance was to the Navy.

Another comment: When students wrote him for his advice or for stories, in connection with their school work, he would always refer them to source material. He said he wasn't going to write their papers for them. He received many many letters from young people.

Final comment: Mr. Cozard said he'd never heard Admiral Nimitz say "Jap," he always referred to them with respect as the Japanese.

This was a comment related to Admiral Gallery's book where he calls the North Koreans "Gooks" or some such word. George was saying that Admiral Nimitz never did that in his conversations.

Now that's all. I don't know if that's of any more value to you or not.

INDEX

for an interview

with

GEORGE E. COZARD

Berkeley, 14-15, 20, 24, 27

Byrd, Admiral Richard E., 53

Denfeld, Admiral Louis E., 4, 14, 26

Eisenhower, General Dwight D., 6

Exercises, 18

Fluckey, Admiral and Mrs. Eugene B., 12-14

Forrestal, James, 54

Golden Gate Cemetery, 37

Horseshoes, 19-20, 44-45

"John Paul Jones", 39

King, Admiral Ernest J., 1

Lee, Robert M., 1-2

Long Island, 29

MacArthur, General Douglas, 18, 55

McCarthy, Daniel, 2-3

Morison, Samuel Eliot, 31

Naval Gun Factory, 1

Nimitz, Mrs. Chester W., 10, 12-14, 19, 31, 33-34, 46-47, 53

Nimitz, Chester W., Jr., 45, 54

Oak Knoll Hospital, 36-37

Pearl Harbor, 21

Pentagon, 4, 6

Potter, Professor E. B., 39, 55

Sea Power, 39

Sproul, Robert and Ida, 12-14

Spruance, Admiral Raymond Ames, 37

Swimming, 29

Texas, 14

Truman, President Harry, 20, 36

Turner, Admiral Kelly, 37

Unification Act, 16

United Nations, 27-28

Walking, 18

Washington, D. C. 1, 6, 14-16, 19-23

Chelsea Naval Hospital,
Chelsea, Mass.

Captain Tracy D. Cuttle, USN
Subject: Admiral Nimitz

by John T. Mason, Jr.
August 28, 1969

Mr. Mason: Captain, it's such a wonderful thing that you've consented to give me some time this morning in your last few hours of your active command here at the Naval Hospital. I was anxious to reach you, however, because I understand that you're going off to Europe on an indefinite kind of tour.

I wonder if you'd begin by telling me, when you first met Admiral Nimitz; then I believe he was Captain Nimitz --

Captain Cuttle: He was Commander Nimitz, and he was professor of Naval Science and Tactics at the University of California at Berkeley. This was the first of the Naval ROTC classes.

Q: It was the prototype of all those to come, was it not?

Cuttle: I think they had six which started at the same time - one at Harvard, Yale, Northwestern, Georgia Tech, Washington, and the University of California.

At that time, everyone was required to have a least two years of military training if they were at the University of California. They had had Army ROTC before, but this was the first Navy ROTC.

Cuttle - 2

Q: It was similar to the plan in effect with land grant colleges in the middle west.

Cuttle: That's correct. Jim Archer and I went down to sign up for our military training. Jim's father had been a Colonel in the Army, and he said, "We certainly don't want to get in the Army."

Q: Let's go in the other direction.

Cuttle: So, we went to a table where, then, Commander Nimitz and Lieutenant Commander Gunther were seated recruiting students for the Naval ROTC. Then, we signed up for that rather than the Army.

We had 50 in the original class, which was really a skeleton platoon. Of course, they had a regiment of Army. Every Friday we had a review, the skeleton platoon with a regiment of Army would pass by the reviewing stand. We were in blues with white gloves. So, any mistake was signaled. We had a bad time to start with.

They took 50 in each class, so by the time we graduated, at least we had a better showing.

During the time I was there, Nimitz made Captain while I was there. He was relieved by Captain Bruce Canaga.

Q: Who was his life-long friend.

Cuttle - 3

Cuttle: Very definitely. The reason that I was able to get in the Naval ROTC, at that time I thought I was going to be an architect, they weren't taking people in pre-med; That first summer I worked for an architect and I decided that I prefered to change. So, they kept me on, even though I was in pre-med after that.

Q: You didn't have the problem that Lattu had. He wasn't a citizen, so he had great difficulty getting enrolled.

Cuttle: That's right. When it came time for our commissioning, Onnie had to get a lot of dental work done before he was accepted dentally. He had worked his way through, and this was quite a problem for him.

Q: Tell me, then, about Captan Nimitz; and how he conducted the classes and that sort of thing.

Cuttle: To start with, there were just the two officers, and four Chief Petty officers. The idea was that we would get most of the courses that were given at the Academy included in our cirriculum. The added ones were Seamanship, Gunnery, Tactics, and so forth. We had to take a course in Navigation and Nautical Astronomy, which was given by one of the civilian professors.

They were perfectly wonderful gentlemen to be associated with. However, we did have quite a number who dropped out. So, our original graduating class was only 14 out of the 50.

Q: They dropped out because it was too rigorous, or what?

Cuttle: For all sorts of reasons. They left med school; they didn't drop out of just the naval program; they dropped out of school entirely.

One of the things that is different about the Navy and the Army is that when we signed up in the Navy, it was for the four year course; while in the Army they only had two years of compulsory training. Then, if they wanted to go ahead and get a commission, they went the other two years.

So, we were graduated Ensigns, deck-volunteer general status.

Q: It was a small enough group that it was almost like a naval family, wasn't it?

Cuttle: Absolutely, yes. There was very close association, not only with the members of the unit, but with the officers. As the numbers grew, additional junior officers were assigned. Even by the time of graduation, not more than maybe a half a dozen, altogether.

After we were commissioned, we were assigned to a fleet division. The sixth fleet division in Oakland was the one that I was assigned to. We had summer cruises.

I was very fortunate, since I had transferred to pre-med I had another year to make up in pre-med courses. Among these, was one in Vertebrate Zoology. The professor in this was interested in getting a collection of bats for comparative study on bats.

About the time that the old CHICAGO was going on a shakedown cruise down to the south Pacific; I was offered an opportunity to go along as a newly commissioned Ensign on this delightful cruise to collect specimins for the professor of Vertebrate Zoology.

Q: That was a pleasant assignment.

Cuttle: It sure was.

Q: Where did it take you?

Cuttle: We went first to Honolulu, then to Tahiti, and Samoa. Then back to Honolulu and San Francisco. I was the only reserve officer aboard. I had a great time.

Between Honolulu and Tahiti, a frigate bird flew into the superstructure. He broke his neck and fell on the deck. This was about three o'clock in the morning. They brought me out to prepare this specimin, which I did. After that, they called me 'one bird Cuttle'.

I got hundreds of bats for Professor GRINELL.

Q: I would have thought you'd have gone as far as New Zealand, to get the bats which are famous down there.

Cuttle: They're in Samoa. There are caves on the on the other side of the Island. They were just filled with bats. I just got pocketsfull.

Q: Were they infected in any way?

Cuttle: No, not rabid. The big — BATS, too, in Samoa. Anyway, I got an A in the course.

Q: Tell me about your relationship with the Nimitz family.

Cuttle: On one of these two-week summer cruises - then Captain Nimitz had the submarine outfit down at San Diego - we called on him. He was, of course very hospitable and we had a lovely time.

I went back to attend the medical school, and I didn't see him again until I was with the Marines in Okinawa. I got a mortar shell in my lap, and was taken to Guam to be patched up.

I don't know how he even knew I was there, but when I was ambulatory, he sent a car down and invited me to dinner at his headquarters.

Q: On Guam?

Cuttle: On Guam. When it came time for me to receive a Purple Heart, he presented it to me at the nine o'clock conference, when all the Admirals in the whole staff were there. It just shows you what a perfectly delightful and thoughtful man he was. This was right in the middle of the Okinawa campaign. He had a lot of things to worry about except a former student at the Naval ROTC.

Q: Apparently he kept in touch with all you fellows for years.

Cuttle: Yes, indeed.

Q: He knew exactly where you were and --

Cuttle: And what we were doing.

Q: In that sense, did you ever feel any evidence of his more than just passing interest in the development of your career? In terms of assignments that might have opened, and so on.

Cuttle: I don't believe so, I don't think that he influenced our assignments. After World War II was over, I came back as Chief of Medicine at the little hospital at Treasure Island until that closed. Then I was transferred to the Naval Hospital in Oakland. After the Admiral -

Q: Is that Oak Knoll?

Cuttle: Yes, the Naval Hospital at Oakland. That was when I first took care of the Admiral, and Mrs. Nimitz. As I was in charge of the sick officers, S.O.Q., and dependents medical service.

Q: That's where she had given all her war-time service.

Cuttle: That's right. She was a volunteer - then called Grey Ladies. During the war, she worked constantly at that Naval Hospital.

This was after the war. He and his life-long friend, Captain Canaga were both patients of mine; sometimes at the same time. He and Captain Canaga took long walks together, practically every day, out in Berkeley. They'd both tell me about all these long walks that they took. I think, he stayed in very good health.

After I left to come to Chelsea the first time when I came here as Chief of Medicine, both of them were fine.

Q: This was before she had arthritis?

Cuttle: Yes, she was doing very well. She had relatives, her sister, who lived at Wellfleet down on the Cape. When she and the Admiral came back to spend the summer with her sister —

Q: Miss Freeman.

Cuttle: Yes. I was invited to come down and go fishing with the Admiral. We had a great time for a couple of days. Fishing for stripped bass.

Then I went from here to Chief of Medicine at the Naval Hospital in Nikko, Japan. Then I didn't see them again until I got back to Oakland.

Although he had aged considerably, and she had developed quite extensive arthritis; they were getting along well.

Q: Was he still taking those long walks?

Cuttle: Yes, I think he was. Captain Canaga, died just a few weeks before the Admiral did. As you know, I was here at that time. I was told about him having a cerebral thrombosis —

Q: He had that very difficult operation a short time before.

Cuttle: Yes. This was long after I had left.

Q: Apparently that was related to a much earlier experience in his career, when he was crushed by something that fell on him or something.

Cuttle: Yes, I don't remember the details of the accident.

Q: As I understand it, it was the pinched cord. The spinal cord was being pinched, or something.

Cuttle: Yes, but I'm not sure that that was related to the previous accident. A   disc is quite common without a preceeding problem.

Even in the end, he was interested and kept in touch with many of us.

Q: You spoke about going fishing with him, did you also get involved with his horseshoe playing?

Cuttle: We used to do that out at Oakland.

Q: Oh, you did. Were you good at that?

Cuttle: Not as good as he was, nowhere near. He was a very fine horseshoe pitcher. In fact, I'm sure that you have pro-

Cuttle - 11

bably seen the picture of the contest that they had there. I think that the picture is still in sort of a wardroom there. Have you seen that?

Q: No, I haven't. I have not been to Oak Knoll.

Cuttle: With the Admiral pitching horseshoes.

Q: Apparently being very proud of the fact that he got various people interested in horseshoe pitching.

Cuttle: Oh, yes, he had this set up in Guam. He had also one of the Japanese telescopes that had been captured. He had it out at his headquarters in Guam. Later when they settled in the hills at Berkeley, and we called on him there. He had this set up so that you could look out all over the San Francisco Bay area. This captured Japanese telescope.

Q: Can you recall any human interest stories about him? Going back even to the NROTC days?

Cuttle: Of course, he had always been an extremely thoughtful gentleman. He put up with a lot of things that make me shudder now.

Q: You say there were some unbelievable things which he put up with at Berkeley.

Cuttle: We, of course, had not been previously exposed to the military; and were, I'm sure, less respectful of rank and rating than we were later.

He had an excellent sense of humor. On one occasion on one of the summer cruises that we took, it was a battleship cruise to Seattle and Victoria. We were getting short of funds, I remember, when we were in Victoria. I had a checking accout, so I wrote this check; and then sent a wire to the bank to transfer funds from the savings account to the checking account to cover the check. Evidentally the wire went astray, because the check bounced. He got a letter of complaint from the Canadian bank. I came in very embarrassed about the whole thing, and explained it to him. He said, "Think nothing of it." He fixed it right up.

I can't think of any other major problems that he got me out of.

Q: Or any scrapes you got into.

Cuttle: The ones I got into, he didn't know about, or didn't bail me out of.

Q: She had you in the home quite often, too, didn't she?

Cuttle: Yes, not only when we were students; but when they settled in Berkeley, we were there on several occasions.

Q: They apparently loved to entertain.

Cuttle: Yes, and did it beautifully.

Q: And part of the entertainment WERE his inevitable stories. Do you remember any of them?

Cuttle: No, I don't off hand. Also, of course, we'd pitch horseshoes. That was included in the entertainment.

Q: You come early enough, before cocktails --

Cuttle: The most thoughtful thing that happened to me was on Guam, when in the midst of the Okinawa campaign, he took the time and trouble to see that I was invited to the best meal that I had all during the war.

Q: It must indicate that he scanned the list of casualities or wounded.

Cuttle: I guess. I don't understand it, because there were scads of wounded. At that time, I was a Lieutenant Commander, Medical Corps Reserve. I was just extremely impressed with that amount of thoughtfullness.

Q: Did he remember important events in your life, as he did some of them? Birthdays, and that kind of thing.

Cuttle: Yes. I don't think he ever remembered my birthday. He used to write a note, whenever I got a new job or new change of duty.

Q: He knew about this.

Cuttle: He knew about it, I don't know how he kept track of all this as well as he did. He certainly was a great man.

Admiral Gunther was also a patient of mine, after World War II, and died with thrombosis. Bronchial carcinoma.

Q: What about Admiral Gunther?

Cuttle: Admiral Gunther; who had been the first Executive Officer, then Lieutenant Commander, was an Admiral, aviation type. He came back as a patient, when I was at Oakland. He died of ~~cardio~~ Bronchial carcinoma.

So, I had a chance at least to take care of both my commanding officers, both professors and assistant professors.

Q: That gave you a certain amount of professional satisfaction.

Cuttle: It sure did.

Cuttle - 15

Q: Have you continued in touch with Mrs. Nimitz?

Cuttle: Only at Christmas time now. We exchange cards and notes. I think last Christmas was the last time I've heard from her.

Q: What about the children - did you get to know them, did you know Chester, Jr?

Cuttle: No, not well at all.

Q: Was he at Berkeley? When they were there?

Cuttle: Yes, he was. Younger, of course I met them, but I didn't really know them. One daughter became a nun.

Q: Yes, Mary. She was a much later child, than the three. I don't think she was born when they were there.

Cuttle: No, there were just three when we were at school there. I hear also frequently from Helen Gunther, Admiral Gunther's widow. She's living in San Francisco. She's been to visit us here, and also when I had the hospital out at Portsmouth, New Hampshire. So, it was still a tight outfit.

Q: There was sort of an alumnus to this school affair.

You said to your friend on the telephone that you thought you might settle in the Bay area. So, I presume you will see Mrs. Nimitz then.

Cuttle: Mrs. Nimitz, and in fact Helen Gunther has asked us to stay with her until we find a place to live. We probably won't do that, but at least she's given us the offer.

We plan to be about ten months going around the world, and end up in San Francisco about July of '70.

Q: A great prospect in this.

Cuttle: We're looking forward to it.

Q: Thank you very much, Captain.

INDEX

for an interview

with

CAPTAIN TRACY D. CUTTLE, U. S. NAVY (MC) (RET.)

Aquinas, Sister Mary (Nimitz) 15

Archer, James, 2

AROTC, 1

California, University of, 1

Canaga, Captain Bruce, 2, 8-9

Chicago, 5

Freeman, Miss Elizabeth, 9

Gringell, Professor, 6

Guam, 6-7, 11, 13

Gunther, LCDR and Mrs., 2, 14-16

Lattu, Admiral Onnie, 3

Nimitz, Mrs. Chester W., 8-9, 12, 15-16

Nimitz, Chester W., Jr., 15

Nimitz, Mary (see Aquinas)

NROTC, Berkeley, 1-3, 7, 11-12

Oak Knoll, 8, 10-11

Okinawa, 6-7, 13

Interview with Judge Charles M. Fox, Jr.

Place: His office at 861 Sixth Avenue, San Diego, California

Date: 17 March 1970

Subject: Fleet Admiral Chester A. Nimitz

By: Professor E. B. Potter

Q: Judge Fox, you were explaining your theory as to why on October 25th 1944 in the Third Fleet the radio messages from Admiral Kinkaid were coming through under so much delay, coming up from Leyte Gulf. Would you tell us your reasoning again?

Judge F.: The reason was that since the Leyte operation had reached the landing stage the radio circuits had become burdened with a great amount of radio traffic which had originated from Army command sources, and putting this information on the Fox Broadcast Schedule from NPM in Honolulu imposed a terrific burden on that schedule because it was transmitted at a fairly low rate of words per minute, because all of the ships in the fleet were expected to copy most of the messages, or at least be able to copy them. Therefore, with this tremendous increase in traffic imposed on this circuit, the time interval increased greatly. It built up rather slowly at first, and then became quite apparent.

We were faced with a situation where it seemed that, in order to get the message out to the fleet, the originators, particularly in the southwest command, were increasing the precedence of the message, and this is a contagious disease that spreads, and the result is that you have a very high percentage of operational priority and urgency messages which ordinarily would not have been in that category.

Q: Do you think there's anything, Judge Fox, to the theory that the Japanese were using their station at Singapore pretending to be the Wasatch, Admiral Kinkaid's flagship?

Judge F.: Well, after difficulties had become apparent insofar as communications with the Wasatch were concerned, we did communicate with the Wasatch, and I recall specifically one instance where afte supposedly delivering a message to the Wasatch, which took some 20 minutes to transmit by hand, that the station to which we were sending the message was unable to authenticate its receipt. It was some time after this that I learned that the Japs had taken a station in Singapore and had for several days, apparently, been interfering in procedural signals with our attempted communications with the Wasatch and their communications with us.

This interference is really more effective than jamming, in that it occupies your operators' time and you're not aware of the fact that it is the enemy which is causing the difficulty. In the case of jamming, you could switch to another frequency. Actually our operators blamed Army personnel they believed to be on the Wasa

Q: Thank you, Judge Fox. Now, I am particularly anxious to get the sequence of events as they occurred aboard the New Jersey on the 25th of October 1944. The message as sent from Pearl Harbor, though we've often forgotten because it's been reworded differently from the files the message as sent, read as follows: "Turkey Trots to water a double letter addresses ComThird Fleet action addressee." The info addressees were CNO and CTF 77, then an X, then the message, "Where is Task Force 34" double letter, then "the world wonders."

Now, when were you first aware that there was something odd about this message, Judge Fox? It came in by electric ciphering machine or electric typing machine?

Judge F.: Yes, it came in and because of the cryptographic channel which was used it was a message which could only have been deciphered by top commands. It was a short message, and because of its precedence - I believe it was an urgent - as soon as it was decoded, it was handed to my assistant, Burton Goldstein...

Q: Who handed it to your assistant? An enlisted man?

Judge F.: No, it would have been an officer who decoded it, and I've never been able to ascertain who did actually decode it. We did have a man by the name of Blum who had been with the FBI and who was one of our top men and I have always thought that he probably was the one, but I am not sure who did it. In any event, Goldstein handed it to me. It was a very short tape. My recollection is that the padding at the end of the message was still on the message when Mr. Goldstein handed it to me. The question was whether to tear it off or not. The tape was very short. It was to be transmitted to flag plot by pneumatic tubes with a cartridge such as department stores would have used, and I told Mr. Goldstein to send it up to flag plot...

Q: After removing the initial padding, "Turkey trots to water"?

Judge F.: That I have no recollection of whatsoever. Insofar as I'm concerned, I'm not aware that I told Mr. Goldstein to remove any padding.

Fox - 4

Q: One of the puzzles about this whole episode is the ability of the officer who received it at the far end of this tube and handed it to Admiral Halsey. He was a liaison officer, was he?

Judge F.: Well, one of the coding officers that was under my jurisdiction was an officer who was assigned to flag plot, and at the other end of this pneumatic tube, in flag plot, he had a typewriter, and in the case where we had written up a message and then sent it up in the tube, he would hand out the dispatch we had typed in Rdo 1.

Q: Let me get one thing straight. What you sent in the tube was the tape just after it came off the deciphering machine?

Judge F.: Absolutely, right. We automatically re-broke the messag in order that the dispatch itself could be written up. That was ou procedure with urgents. In this case, I am not sure that at that point we actually did re-break it and write it up because of the personal nature of the message. But the liaison officer that I referred to before was a man who was familiar with our procedures and who was at the other end of the pneumatic tube. In addition to tha there was a Lieutenant Don Kennedy who had been in communications, who, subsequently, had become, for want of a better term, an aide t Admiral Carney, who was chief of staff at that time.

Now, as to what happened to the message after it got to flag plot, I have never been able to determine.

Q: Normally, you would suppose that the officer who handed it to Admiral Carney, or Admiral Halsey, would point out that there was a double letter before "The world wonders" and suggest that it might be padding, wouldn't you think?

Fox - 5

Judge F.: Well, yes. I can't be sure, but I would be very much surprised if the message was handed directly to Admiral Halsey, but I wasn't there and I don't know. It's entirely possible that in the confusion they neglected to point out that there was padding. But the point that I have wanted to make throughout this, is that the message typed on a dispatch form, such as we used for all our messages, as typed up by communications, was never typed up with the padding in it as a part of the message. That was part of our job when we typed up messages. We deleted the padding.

Q: There still remains a little air of mystery about it that I supposed will be never quite solved, because, of course, when Admiral Halsey became so excited and threw his hat on the floor and said something in his own words that I was ashamed to have said, and Admiral Carney -- Captain Carney then - said, "Control yourself, Bill, control yourself. Come on now." With all of that going on, you'd think somebody would try to explain it, wouldn't you?

Judge F.: I think, as I pointed out before, to my mind, the fact that Admiral Nimitz was asking Admiral Halsey where the battleships of the task force were, was a sufficient reprimand of itself, if you want to call it a reprimand. This, to my mind, was - would have shocked Admiral Halsey of itself because it indicated there was a missing link that shouldn't have been possible - or at best an ambiguity in the orders issued by ComThird Fleet.

Q: Particularly since the message specified Admiral King and Admiral Kinkaid as the info addressees.

Judge F.: That's true, and I have always thought that far too much emphasis was placed on this padding part of that message.

Fox - 6

Q: But, of course, you know who placed the emphasis, don't you?

Judge F.: Well, I can only guess.

Q: It's hard to say. You've read Admiral Halsey's story, of course?

Judge F.: Yes.

Q: And who was it wrote with him on that, his ghost writer?

Judge F.: Bryant?

Q: That's it. He evidently had Admiral Halsey's acquiescence, but it builds up to a climax with the message, "Where is Lee. Send Lee" and there never was any such message, as you know. Certainly not just before this task force 34 message. But it makes a good story.

Judge F.: There was a plain language broadcast about Admiral Lee. I believe it said "Send Lee with fast battleships etc." or something like that.

Q: But it was much earlier and it wasn't worded like that.

Judge F.: Oh, no. But I recall that distinctly, and oddly enough, it turns out that that plain language broadcast, which shocked us at the time to receive it, probably had an effect on the Japanese task force to make them conclude that we were very close.

Q: You're quite right about that. But the two incorrect things about it are the wording and the timing, which the files show are quite wrong in both instances. I think there's a little drama mixed up in this thing that isn't necessarily representing the truth. Of course, all Admiral Nimitz said is "Ask him where Task Force 34 is."

And Admiral Austin was the one who put the "repeat" in there, and the ensign down below put the padding on.

Judge F.: Well, the message would have needed to be longer than the simple four-worded, "Where is Task Force 34?" I think the cryptographic requirements would have required that the message be longer than that. So I would place no emphasis on the "repeat," that is, to my mind. I would be surprised if Admiral Halsey assumed that the "repeat" was a part of the reprimand or whatever you want to call it. I didn't understand it that way. Repeat was used constantly in dispatches. In fact the frequent use was criticized

Q: I'm a little weak, it's been years since I had anything to do with communications. Didn't you sometimes make a repeat just to make sure a word that had got garbled would come through correctly and be understood?

Judge F.: That's perfectly true, and that's also a reason why you cannot always assume that two nulls that separate padding from a message are not another word, because sometimes, due to transmission errors or decoding errors, it is entirely possible that that was a word.

Q: That's perfectly true. It could be "as," for example, "As the world wonders." Nevertheless, weren't you required by Admiral Halsey or somebody to break that message several more times?

Judge F.: We broke that message innumerable times, and it was available in the re-broken version when Admiral Nimitz came down at Christmas of that year. We broke that message several times.

Q: Of course, in Admiral Halsey's story, it says that when Admiral

Nimitz got back to Pearl Harbor, he traced the little so-and-so down and chewed him up. Well, that isn't what happened, of course. He simply said to Captain Redman, "Remove him to a less sensitive spot."

Judge F.: Well, I think it was a problem at times actually to think of padding to put in a message. An ensign or someone is handed an urgent message from Admiral Nimitz or Admiral Halsey and he's told to do it right away, and I don't know what their procedure was, who wrote the padding in, but in any event, under those circumstances, sometimes padding got in that had some relation to it. It conceivably could have relation to a message. It was kind of a hard thing to police. (see letter 6/2

Q: Yes, it certainly was. Have you anything else that you would like to add about that particular receipt?

Judge F.: I don't think in addition to what I've said before to you and what I've said today.

Q: Judge Fox, it is our policy in preparing transcripts on these recordings to send them to the person interviewed for any corrections he chooses to make. Your address is 861 Sixth Street, San Diego.

Judge F.: I think it would be better to use 561 San Fernando, San Diego, 92106.

Q: Thank you

DECLARATION OF TRUST

The undersigned does hereby appoint and designate as his (her) Trustee herein, the Secretary-Treasurer and Publisher of the United States Naval Institute to perform and discharge the following duties, powers, and privileges in connection with the possession and use of a certain taped interview between the undersigned and the Oral History Department of the United States Naval Institute.

(1) As an <u>Open</u> transcript it may be read (or the tape audited) by qualified researchers upon presentation of proper credentials as determined by the Trustee. In the case of interviews about the late Fleet Admiral C. W. Nimitz, it is intended that first use of the material shall be made by the biographer of the Fleet Admiral, Professor E. B. Potter, and the Naval Institute is authorized to deal with the material in this fashion.

(2) It is expressly understood that in giving this authorization, I am in no way precluded from placing such restrictions as I may desire upon use of the interview at any time during my lifetime, nor does this authorization in any way affect my rights to the copyright of any literary expressions that may be contained in the interview.

Witness my hand and seal this 30th day of May 19 70.

Allen G. Quynn

I hereby accept and consent to the foregoing Declaration of Trust and the powers therein conferred upon me as Trustee.

R. E. Bowker Jr.
Secretary-Treasurer and Publisher

- 1 - Interview # 1

Rear Admiral Allen G. Quynn, USN, Ret. by John T. Mason, Jr.
Frederick, Maryland December 17, 1969
Subject: Admiral Nimitz

Mr. Mason: Admiral, you had such a splendid opportunity during your five years of service in the Pacific to know Admiral Nimitz as a person. I wonder if you would recall for me some of your recollections about that man.

As you know, we're gathering information in preparation for a biography of the Admiral. The official record is very voluminous, but the personal record is not quite so. We have been trying to reach men who knew him and knew him in a personal way.

Admiral Quynn: I wrote an article on it here:
"I believe Admiral Chester W. Nimitz was one of America's greatest war leaders.
"Nimitz, said Admiral Quynn, was sent to replace Admiral Husband A. Kimmel as Commander in Chief of the Pacific after the Japanese attack that left the main United States base in the Pacific a shambles.
"In my opinion, the greatest victory under Nimitz was the battle of Midway in June 1942. The Japanese didn't think we knew they were planning a major operation there. The Admiral

#1 Quynn - 2

threw everything he had into the fight. I'll never forget how we all sweated that out in Pearl Harbor.

"Admiral Nimitz was a forceful person. He never sought publicity. He was very canny, tactful, and stuck to his post 24 hours a day.

"In Pearl Harbor, Admiral Nimitz was a bug on physical fitness. He used to play horseshoes daily to relieve his tension. I was pretty good at it too, but could rarely beat him.

"The last time I saw Admiral Nimitz was in 1955 at the Naval Academy in Annapolis, when he attended the 50th anniversary of the class of 1905."

Q: All right sir, now will you put some flesh on the bones. Tell me, did you know him before he came out to Pearl to take over?

Quynn: No.

Q: That was your first meeting with him?

Quynn: That's right.

I've got a wonderful picture there showing many top leaders in the Pacific. I don't know whether you want to use that in some capacity, but I'll show it to you in a few minutes. It was taken on the occasion of Admiral Calhoun, Commander Service Force, giving a luncheon for the senior officers present at Pearl Harbor.

#1 Quynn - 3

Q: This was just within weeks after Nimitz had taken over.

Quynn: That's right. The Admirals who were in the top posts, at that time, got together in his quarters and we had a dinner where we sort of tried to build up our morale a little bit and talk over what we were going to do. It wasn't formal, but it was a chance to get together on the problems that we had to face.

From then on, I knew Admiral Nimitz quite intimately. There were many people more senior than I working with him. I actually wasn't on his staff, except the Service Force was under him directly. I was number two in the Service Force.

Q: At that point the total staff out there was fairly small, wasn't it?

1 Quynn - 4

Quynn: Yes.

Q: So, it was a family sort of thing.

Quynn: That's right.

In other words, before Pearl Harbor the PENNSYLVANIA was the fleet flag ship. But before Pearl Harbor they had moved ashore to the submarine, base that is Admiral Kimmel had with his staff.

The Service Force was still on the ARGONNE. Shortly after Pearl Harbor we moved ashore to Kuahua Island, which was a little island in the middle of Pearl Harbor where the ammunition depot used to be.

Then after both Admiral Nimitz's staff and the Service Force staff expanded, we had to look for new quarters. The fleet built a heavily protected concrete quarters, which I think they still use now, ashore. The lower floor had six feet of concrete and that's where all the secret publications were contained. The upper floor was protected, but not as strong. So

The Service Force had offices in this building, but they expanded so much that we had to build another building equally large right next to it. That's where we were the rest of the war.

In other words, CincPac had his own heavily constructed building. Ours was simply frame; we were just taking a chance on somebody not dropping a bomb on us.

That was the setup during the whole war until we got so far advanced across the Pacific that they felt that the Commander in Chief of the Pacific Fleet, Admiral Nimitz, ought to be nearer the scene of the action. So then, they established his headquarters on Guam. Admiral Nimitz and the combatant part of his staff moved out there. They left Admiral Towers back as Commander of Pacific Ocean areas. The Service Force still stayed back there, except we had dozens of advance bases.

One of the things that the Service Force had was an advance base section. There are so many things I could talk about, I don't when to stop.

Q: If you'd concentrate on Nimitz first, then we'll do the other in detail.

Quynn: Admiral Nimitz was there, but he frequently went out to the advance areas. He'd fly out to see how the situation was and so forth. Then he got to the point where he felt he ought to be closer to the scene of action, so they established the advance headquarters at Guam.

1 Quynn - 6

Q: Was it necessary for Admiral Nimitz to make all these flying trips to islands? I mean, it was a dangerous mission always, wasn't it?

Quynn: Not exactly. The Commander in Chief of anything can't be sitting back where he's well protected and not in direct contact with what's going on.

Of course, at his headquarters in Pearl Harbor we'd have these conferences every morning where the representatives of all the branches of the services - Admiral Nimitz and his staff and the General at Honolulu (Short was there at the time of Pearl Harbor, this was his successor) [Emmons] - at nine o'clock in the protected area down there, when his Chief of Staff would give a run down on what took place in the preceeding 24 hours.

Another thing that doesn't have anything to do with the Service Force, but with a change in tactics. When we realized that it was going to be a carrier war, he brought in Admiral Sherman to be his ~~Chief of Staff~~ [Operations Officer]. Because he was more familiar with carriers than they were.

Q: When did that realization come?

Quynn: I would say it came about the time of the battle of Midway. At the time of the battle of Midway Admiral Davis, who was a classmate of mine, was Admiral Nimitz's air officer. He directed, under Admiral Nimitz, the distribution and operation of all and every aircraft that was available in that area.

I remember talking to him several times during that period. When he had to send in these torpedo planes, which he knew very few if any of them were coming back. Out of 16 they sent in, one came back.

What we should have had were bombers to soften up the Japanese anti-aircraft. Then send in the torpedo planes. But the torpedo planes had to go in without that coverage.

Q: They were very vulnerable.

Quynn: They were very slow. But anyway they sank four Japanese carriers.

So those are the things that went on around Midway.

Q: You said a few minutes ago, you suffered through this preparation for Midway at Pearl Harbor. Tell me about his reactions.

Quynn: I can't say that I was really sitting beside him. But I was working with his staff and talking with them in seeing what we could do to support their force. For instance,

We knew there were going to be some ships sunk. (Later on in the war we had this salvage organization, one with each squadron.) We had big powerful fleet tugs that could go out and tow a big ship in at seven or eight knots. At that time, we only had a few of them.

When the YORKTOWN was damaged we sent out the VIREO, which was a World War I mine sweeper, to tow in the YORKTOWN at a speed of three knots. Of course we knew she was never going to get back; submarines I believe caught up with her and that was it.

We were working with them all the time to see what facilities we could send out to support. We knew what was going to happen at the battle of Midway.

Q: Facing up to a crucial battle like that, and with the circumstances being what they were, what was his mood?

Quynn: I'd say he was very calm and collected. That's the way he was all the time; just like Spruance was. He realized the seriousness of it.

We knew ahead of time, four or five days, that the attack was going to be on Midway. Midway was 1100 miles from Pearl Harbor. Everything that could shoot, or bomb or torpedo, or do anything, we either got out there on a ship or on the land.

There are several wonderful books on that subject. I've got both of them here right now. One of the books that I don't have is one where they kill a Japanese Admiral. You've read that, haven't you?

Q: Yes.

The reason I ask you is because one of the things the biographer is really interested in finding out is how Admiral Nimitz reacted at the time of these various crucial battles.

Quynn: I'd say he was very calm and collected. The two or three days just preceeding Midway, I probably didn't see him at all. But I did work with a lot of his staff.

Captain Steele is mentioned in this book I have. He is mentioned a number of times. He was his operations officer. Then of course when they went over to the air officers being operations officers, Steel lost his job.

Q: Not being a Pensacola boy.

Quynn: That's right.

That showed that Admiral Nimitz had a lot of vision. He knew that the rest of the war was going to be primarily an air war.

As you know, Admiral Spruance was in several big engagements where the fleets never saw each other. He had to depend on his air officer, I don't know who he had at that time, to decide when the planes should be sent out and and when they should be brought in and what the capacity was and things of that kind.

Admiral Nimitz had foresight. The line officers didn't like it very much. (You don't necessarily have to emphasize that.) They felt that with the handling of the ships, they were more capable than the naval aviators who through their early career had never handled ships.

I know that from personal experience. I was on a number of ships where we had naval aviators. They couldn't stand a night watch on the ship, because they were going to get up and fly in the morning. Of course they'd have been better off if they had learned to handle the ships.

Q: Tell me about the Admiral's morning conferences.

#1 Quynn - 11

In the conference room

Quynn: He had a big map ~~up there~~ showing the whole area of operations. His operations officer, or war plans officer was Lynn McCormick. He was head of my class for many years. He figures in this book I was telling you about very frequently. So does Captain Steele, and Captain (later Admiral) Davis. They were all contemporaries of mine and friends of mine. Those were the people that I used to talk to about these things.

I do remember during the beginning of the battle of Midway, it lasted two or three days all told, I know that Admiral Nimitz was very calm and collected. He was taking everything as seriously as anybody could in consulting with all these people I'm telling you about as to what the next move should be or what we could do.

In the matter of the YORKTOWN, there was nothing we could do about it. There it was, and we had nothing suitable to tow it out with any great speed only this poor VIREO that went about three knots. He'd never get there.

Q: Do you recall any special morning sessions as standing out?

Quynn: One thing, I've told this a number of times, and he probably told it too. I forget exactly what the situation was at the time.

A Congressional Committee was out there and one of the members was Senator Margaret Chase Smith of Maine. We had this Committee in there and Adm. Nimitz was explaining to them what the problems were in the Pacific. He had this large map that covered a whole wall.

He said, "You see how the Pacific is; how big it is. You can't get from one place to another in a few minutes or a few hours or anything like that. In fact, the Pacific is almost as big as Texas." That got a big laugh out of the Committee. Adm. Nimitz of course was from Texas.

That was one of the things he told from time to time. He was great on story telling. I used to know a lot of his stories, but I can't remember them now. That wasn't a story really; it was just his explanation of how things were out there. And what our problems were; there were thousands and thousands of miles that we had to cover to get any place.

One of the logistic situations that we had which was very interesting was a question of fuel supply. You can't get fuel from Aruba, down in South America, to the middle of the Pacific in five minutes. Months ahead of time, when one campaign was completely over, we'd have to get bulk carriers loaded for the next campaign. They picked up the oil at Aruba or wherever they were getting it from, in that case they Transited the Canal and came over here to the fleet tankers. They would transfer the fuel from the bulk tankers to the fleet tankers. And they in turn would fuel the fleet at sea.

So at times we had situations where the fleet, the third fleet or the fifth fleet, never got in touch with land for six weeks at a time. All of the fuel, all of the ammunition, all the prov~~divisions~~, everything was transferred at sea by our tankers or by our ammunitions ships, or by repair ships, in some cases, or by provision ships.

Q: A complete floating supply train.

Quynn: That's right, that's what it was. Whenever the fleet went in to an action, in the later years in the war when they had gotten things organized, this force would be right behind them, maybe 100 miles or something like that.

I don't know how many people know these things, but I knew them at the time. Admiral Spruance ~~was~~ would be in command of the whole operation, all the Marines and the Army and so forth, until they were safely landed. When the senior one, the Marine or the Army officer, felt that they had secured the island, he would say, "I will take command."

Then Admiral Spruance and his force would draw back, and refuel and everything else. We did everything; we even had mail delivered to them back there.

Q: This supply train must have been fairly vulnerable to Jap subs or Jap planes, wasn't it?

Quynn: No, there weren't many. We had superiority in planes and everything towards the end there.

I was telling this story the other night about Admiral Spruance. This was only a few weeks after we captured Kwajalein. Kwajalein was about half way across. By that time we had the Japs pretty well subdued.

I was out there on an inspection to Kwajalein and Einawetok. They were two places that we took at the same time. That night Admiral Spruance knew I was there and he invited me over to have dinner on his flag ship, the NEW JERSEY. Here we sat in this enormous atoll, mayby 30 or 40 miles across. The whole fleet - battleships, carriers, cruisers, and every other kind of ship imaginable - anchored there with their lights on in the middle of the Pacific. He evidentally knew that we had the Japs so much under control that there was nothing they could do. I don't say they didn't have anti-submarine patrol and things like that.

Q: But in the earlier period, did the Japs ever make an attempt on the supply trains?

Quynn: Very little, for some reason or other. We could never understand it. Except in the early days of the war, when they sank one tanker, as I remember, right off of Pearl Harbor 20 or 30 miles.

1 Quynn - 15

Once or twice they dropped a scattered bomb on Pearl Harbor. That's the nearest they ever did to coming back and repeating the attack.

Q: Did they have the same system for supplying their fleet?

Quynn: I don't know, I can't tell you. They must have had something similar.

Q: Because if they did have the same system, then they must have realized how strategic it was.

Quynn: That's something I can't tell you. I don't know whether they did or not.

Of course we had this salvage organization. A very good friend of mine was in command of that. They would go in right behind, particularly at Okinawa. They had ~~these~~ salvage ships that went in behind the landing forces. They were fitted with all kinds of tugs and things like that, so that if any landing force ship would get into trouble they'd tow them out. To make the matter ~~easier~~ worse, we had typhoons there which didn't help the situation any.

Q: Those were Halsey's typhoons, weren't they?

Quynn: No, this was on Okinawa.

Then we had hospital ships, in lead of this support force. We had small hospital ships that went right behind the landing craft. They had emergency equipment on board, to take the people that were injured and put them on the beach. Then give them first aid and take them out to the hospital ship. All of these things were planned; it was really an enormous thing toward the end.

Q: It really was perfected as a system.

Quynn: Oh yes. All this is written up in that book I told you about. I won't say a few of us did it, but a few of us knew all about it. We discussed it before we did it.

I don't know whether you want this on here or not, about the day of Pearl Harbor. Sunday morning was a beautiful day. I wasn't on the ship at the time; I was on there about 15 minutes later. Of course, I saw half of the ships being sunk and blown up and two or three other things like that. As the day progressed, we got this rain.

The Japanese had come in behind a weather front, so we couldn't pick up their planes. We probably wouldn't have picked them up anyway, because our scouting patrol was very limited.

That night all these ships were either sinking or turning over or doing something. Captain Steele, whom I mentioned before, was in command of the UTAH. UTAH was one of the ships that capsized with three or four hundred aboard. When he went over and satisfied himself that there was nothing more that could be done for them, he reported to the ARGONNE where we were trying to hold the pieces together. We weren't bombed or anthing, because the ARGONNE was not a ship of any importance except as a flag ship.

Capt. Steele came aboard, out of a job. We were looking for tugs and pumps and all kinds of salvage equipment. We decided we'd organize a salvage organization right now, and you're in command of it - Jim Steele. He really started the salvage organization that later lifted all the ships there. Of course, he got out of it very quickly because he didn't have any special qualifications. Anyway, he was responsible for bringing together such salvage equipment as we did have.

A lot of these ships, you couldn't tell if they were going to sink down. They were sitting on coral pinnacles. They were sinking all the time. They were afraid they were going to turn over. So the few tugs we had were pushing against them to hold them against Ford Island, where they were tied up.

All of these tie in with the building up of the service force functions, which later were conducted to a very great extent.

1 Quynn - 18

Q: Going back to Nimitz again, tell me about your recreation with him.

Quynn: I used to play tennis with him. He was a tennis player and he was just a few doors from me.

Q: Did he do that during the war? I thought he was prohibited from playing tennis?

Quynn: Oh no. He didn't play strenous tennis, but he played doubles. I was a fairly good tennis player, and several others were around there. As a matter of fact, the service force built the courts that we played on. That was another little service that we had.
There's a place that was named after me, that's in Pearl Harbor.

Q: The theater?

Quynn: Yes. That's where the planes came in, right over top of that theater. That theater wasn't there at the time,

Q: The theater was used for what?

Quynn: That was the enlisted men's open air movie theater. They had another one similar to that, open air, for the officers up on *Makalapa*. They used to hold church services at both of those places.

Q: Did Admiral Nimitz ever come down to the enlisted men's movies?

Quynn: Oh yes, he often went down. There wasn't anything to do down there, between when they had fighting, except the movies.

I will say the situation that I was in and the other top people were in, they were pretty comfortable when they were not out on a ship. Admiral Nimitz very seldom went to sea. He'd fly out of course.

In other words, when we captured Tarawa for instance, that was the first big place we captured. He'd fly out and see what damage was done and how the Japanese defenses stood up and so forth. At Tarawa, we thought we'd damaged the Japanese defenses considerably. Then when we went in the Japanese just crawled out, and we had terrible loses there.

Then we created a Tarawa on an isolated place on Oahu and *simulated* what we'd done to destroy these pillboxes and so forth. They bombed them and shelled them and did everything else to them. They put animals inside there. When all this was over, they went in and inspected the animals. They were just as happy as they ever were.

So they had to do something else. The only way that they could really get to those pillboxes was right at the entrance to them with different types of flame throwers and things of that kind that were more effective. You couldn't do that until after you landed.

We never did get to the point where they destroyed the Japanese efforts to fight on any of the islands, even on Guam or Saipan, and certainly not on Okinawa. Those are the things I'm sure are in naval history.

Q: Yes, they are.

You said you played tennis with the Admiral. You also played horseshoes with him.

Quynn: That's about all the recreation he had.

Q: Did he go swimming?

Quynn: Yes, he was quite an enthusiastic swimmer. We had a very nice swimming pool there. Admiral Towers had built that, very fancy. He used that.

1 Quynn - 21

He was not for going out socially very much, except for a small group of his friends.

That was the sad part of poor Admiral Kimmel, the criticism they gave him. He never went anyplace, except to have dinner with one or two people and come home at ten o'clock. They had some implications that he had been drinking the night before Pearl Harbor. There was no ~~proof~~ *truth* in that at all.

Q: He just wasn't social. Mrs. Kimmel wasn't there?

Quynn: No, Mrs. Nimitz wasn't there either.

Q: Of course, after Pearl Harbor there was excuse for it.

Quynn: At lot of the officers had their wives out there. I had mine out there for a few months; she was there at Pearl Harbor. I didn't see her for about four or five days. I didn't sit down for about three days either.

With the situation around there, I've described this. I don't know if this fits into the picture but Frederick is the home of Francis Scott Key. He wrote the STARSPANGLED BANNER. Anyway he saw nothing compared to what we saw on the night of Pearl Harbor.

Particularly the whole harbor was aflame. We saw our whole *Fleet* of ships spread all over the harbor, all smoking or burning or something like that. The CALIFORNIA was the ship that was right across from where we were. She had her flag still flying from the quarterdeck. You could see this flag just obscured by the smoke. The smoke would clear away, and you'd see the flag. The flames would leap up and almost obscure it again. Sights like that were far more impressive than they had down ~~here~~ in Baltimore, but nobody thought to write about it.

Q: That was a different age too.

Quynn: That night was a complete nightmare. Adm. Halsey's planes came in and we thought they were Japanese planes. They shot down a couple of them, not very many, about as many of those as they did the Japanese.

Have you seen that book of Navy pictures? You probably have that, I guess. One was this destroyer blew up; I just happened to turn around and the thing just went up.

Q: I have a very vivid picture in my mind of Pearl Harbor. Admiral Nimitz, himself, told me about it when he arrived.

That's an excellent picture.

Quynn: I've got the names on the back, I don't know whether you want it, or give it to the Naval Institute some time.

Q: We could duplicate that, if you would like us to. We could duplicate that for our library.

Quynn: I really think it's a very historic picture. It was taken in early '42, in January.

Q: Tell me some more about the Service Force, sir. Tell me about the basic principle which was established early. You mentioned it earlier to me.

Quynn: I would say the basic principle was to supply the combat forces with everything they needed, when they needed it. In addition to that after they had completed a campaign and captured certain bases then it was up to us to build the bases to whatever Admiral Nimitz, or whoever it was, prescribed, either with mobile equipment or shore based equipment.

For instance - When we went to Guam, Guam had a very poor harbor. It was small with a lot of rocks and everything.

Among the other things that the service force had under it's control, there were a hundred seabee battalions, with a thousand men each. So that was a few people there.

One battalion was called a harbor stretcher battalion. In other words, they would go into a harbor and they would stretch the harbor. They'd blow up the rocks and dredge it.

We had one when we went to Guam. I think that was the first one. It was a big job. We had this 301st battalion. They went out and cleared out the harbor, built breakwaters around it. Some of the old ships were used for breakwaters. Guam ended up by having a large, good size clear harbor with all kinds of docks and facilities and so forth done by the service force.

The thing is that all this was planned by the advanced base section, before we ever got near Guam. We just assumed that it was scheduled that we were going to capture Guam and that we'd need a good harbor there.

So all this was planned by Captain Eccles.

When I got him, they didn't have any advanced base section at all. He was on duty with me in Washington. He was in the advanced base section in Washington. So I got him to come out and put him in command of the advanced base section of the service force. He had a lot of imagination. He had a lot of civil engineers and people like that on his staff.

When they went into any place like that, they knew exactly what they were going to build and how they were going to build it and where the equipment was coming from. Guam was the most outstanding one because that's where CincPac advanced headquarters were going to be. That was planned too. All that was tied together.

I won't say it was done by just pressing a button, but it

was done in reasonably good time and they knew how they were going to do it.

Q: You told me earlier that one of the basic principles was that in large measure it should be a mobile force.

Quynn: Whenever we knew we were only going to be a short time, everything was mobile. It was ready to move.

That is anything that went out with service squadron ten, that Mick Carney was in command of, was a mobile squadron. He had nothing that couldn't be towed. He didn't take anything in that he'd build ashore. Whenever the fleet had captured a base, he tried to have his squadron tagging in behind, and bring in all the facilities. In other words, he'd have a post office in there in a couple of days, and all kind of facilities, and communication facilities with communication ships. It was all mapped out.

I don't know whether you've heard of the advanced base section in the Navy Department. It was just like a Sears Roebuck catalog. If you wanted a small hospital, you'd order an N-1, to go with this outfit that was going in. That was a portable hospital, say 50 beds, and all the equipment.

If you wanted a big base, you ordered a Lion. That was the largest thing they had. That was probably about 10,000 personnel with all the equipment - an airfield and everything else you needed for an advanced base. You'd order this from this advanced base catalog, like a Sears Roebuck catalog. They were assembled on the west coast at Waunamee near San Francisco.

Q: This was all predicated on an optimistic forecast, wasn't it?

Quynn: It was predicated that we were going to do what we planned to do. There was never one place that we said we were going to capture that we didn't capture. We lost a lot of people doing it.

Until we started by-passing certain places, like Truk, we were going to capture at one time. Then we got this island jumping; Adm Sherman had a lot to do with that. He said there was no point in capturing all these islands, you need just the key ones.

They coined this term, I'd never heard it before, we would interdict them. In other words, we would put them in such a condition that they couldn't do anything, that they couldn't move, they were there. When we had a little spare time, we would go back. They used to play dirty tricks on them, they'd spray all their gardens with poisoned gas or something - not a nice thing.

Q: Your term 'interdict' is a good term, taken from the middle ages. Of course it pertained to the church. The Pope interdicted a country or a city, or something and it was shut off.

Quynn: All we did was by-pass. We took the key places that we knew we had to have. We knew we'd control these others so that they couldn't be utilized for any other purposes. Then when we got a little spare time, we'd go back and interdict them a little bit more.

Q: Who made up this catalog you talk about in the Department?

Quynn: We had an advanced base section in the Navy Department. When I was back there in the logistic department, in '43, the advanced base section was more or less under us. They got out this catalog that I'm telling you about. It was pretty thick. It had all these different things.

If you wanted it for a particular operation, a lion for instance down in the Admiralty Islands. Commodore Jimmie Bogue took it down; it was a big advanced base.

Down there, amongst other things, they had an 80,000 ton drydock, ten sections of 8,000 tons each that they towed across the Pacific.

Q: Floating drydock.

Quynn: That's right. They got it over there and welded these sections together. They had an 80,000 ton drydock that could dock any ship in the Navy. I don't know how much they used that.

I went down in one of my experiences, before they captured the Philippines. We had a big service force, and [Gen.] MacArthur had a relatively small one. So we had a conference down at this lion, this advanced base in the Admiraltys, with his staff, to determine what he was going to need to get into the Philippines and what we were going to provide for him that he didn't have. We had a meeting with his staff down there. Our fleet supply officer and I went down there representing CincPac. They had their representatives there. We spent about two weeks down there planning what we were going to furnish him.

Q: Did the General, himself, come in on it?

Quynn: Oh no, he never got down. His Chief of Staff was there.

It just showed the area that the service force covered We had these 300 planes you'd see around there. They weren't fighting planes. They were planes that towed targets.

One fellow who was rather enthusiastic went into General MacArthur's territory. When Admiral Nimitz heard about that, he ordered him back. There was a little bamboo fence in there that you weren't supposed to cross.

Q: Was there any tension between those two commanders?

Quynn: That's another thing about Admiral Nimitz, he had a policy that everybody had to get along together or we wouldn't win the war.

He had the Army under him, he had the Marines under him, and he had the naval aviators under him. That was the first little clash. Because of the smart line officers that he had on his staff; one was Sock McMorris. He was easy to get along with too, but it was hard for him to understand why they'd take some naval aviator who had not had much experience in handling ships and bring him up and put in his job or his advisor's job.

Admiral Nimitz said, "We've got to get along together. We've got to use everything we have to the best use we can place it."

That applied to the Army aviators. That was one of the sad things, especially in the early days. They didn't know anything about navigation. They would go out and drop a lot of bombs and maybe wouldn't even hit the islands.

They'd come back and report so many Japanese cruisers sunk and a Japanese battleship gone. In the next few days, the ~~things~~ *ships* would appear on the ocean.

I remember Admiral Nimitz told one of the top people one time, "I've got to know what you've done, because I can't plan my campaign if three or four cruisers that I thought were sunk or a battleship or so are still afloat. I've got to change my tactics a little bit." (Words to that effect.)

That was one of his basic things, that we all had to work together. And that's what we did. They did it more than Eisenhower did, I think, in Europe.

We had a lot of Army aviators there. It wasn't a separate corps then. It was the Army Air Force. He worked with them, and just told them what they had to do. And that we had to know about what they had done and so forth.

That was another one of his outstanding characteristics, that you had to get people to work together.

Q: Only a quiet patient type man could have done this, I would think.

QUynn: Exactly. He had that.

Just like Eisenhower. I don't think he was any great tactical General, but he had the same facilities of getting people to work together. Incidentially, he was a classmate of mine at West Point. His class at West Point did much better than my class at the Naval Academy.

I don't want to repeat these things, but that is important. That Admiral Nimitz wanted to get everybody to work together, understand the others' problems, and not make claims that they couldn't justify and things of that kind.

Q: Did you see evidence of this cropping out at these morning conferences?

Quynn: Oh yes.

Another character that we had out there most of the time was Holland Smith, the head Marine out there.

Q: He wasn't very adept at getting along with other people, was he?

Quynn: Yes, he was. He had fights with different people, but he got along very well with the Navy

The main trouble we had, say when you have two division of Marines and three divisions of Army on a certain island, we had a time table. They had to go so many miles in so many days or something like that. The Army didn't like to move as fast as the Marines did.

We had to pull out one of the Army divisions. They were going up to Guam, or wherever it was, and the Marines were up here and the Army was back here. They all had to be on the same line. That was about the only trouble, that wasn't Smith's trouble particularly. That was the plan.

Q: The Marines simply moved faster.

Quynn: And took higher casualties, too.

There again, Smith was the most tender hearted person. When he had heard of so many hundreds of Marines being killed during an operation, he was very broken up about it.

Q: How did Nimitz react to that kind of thing, the loss of men?

Quynn: He took it just like Admiral Spruance. He felt that it had to be done.

You don't realize that we had planned these campaigns months ahead of time. For instance - Kwajalein was scheduled for a certain date, and Einawetok a week later. When it took longer to capture Kwajalein than we thought it was going to take, here we had thousands of men embarked on ships out in the middle of the Pacific not doing anything.

In other words, it sort of overlapped. It took 30 days to capture Kwajalein, and a couple of days after that we started on Einawetok and so forth. Finally, everything was timed. You can see it was bad, they had men onboard ship not doing anything.

Q: It would be awfully hard on their morale.

Quynn: That's right, terrible. They weren't too comfortable.

I knew all this by just being in the service force, where everything that somebody did depended somewhat on us. I wasn't in on the planning of these details, or the fighting or anything like that.

Q: It has been said, Admiral, that in previous conflicts — in wars logistics was never looked upon as an imperative part of the whole thing. Would you talk about that a little?

Quynn: The only answer I can give to that is that in this war, particularly in the Pacific, the distances were so great and the needs for so many different things were so great that they couldn't do anything without them.

Most of the small wars in the past, even the Napoleanic Wars which were not small but the distances were relatively small, they didn't have to plan where they were going to get food so much ahead of time or their ammunition requests. They didn't use the term; they had to have logistics of course.

That term wasn't really created until World War II. All of a sudden it became a vital thing.

Another experience that I had - I was up at the Quebec conference; the Trident conference in Quebec.

Q: Was that the first one?

Quynn: No, the third one. President Roosevelt was there and Churchill was there. Of course the British Navy and Army were represented, and our Army and Navy were represented. Admiral King was up there.

I was supposed to be the logistic representative, but it got too big. They sent Badger up, who was my boss, and a lot of other people before we got through with it.

That's where we planned the occupation of Europe - OVERLORD. That was in August of one year, and it didn't start until June of the following year.

That just shows that the things they had to have were tremendous. The artificial breakwaters was a big deal there. They had all kinds of breakwaters. That was one of the problems I was in on.

Q: British mulberrys?

Quynn: Yes. The big round old concrete things and old ships, if they could find any. They even tried out what the Oil Companies used to use, what they call a bubble breakwater. They'd stretch these pipes, use hoses and put holes in them and put compressed air in them, to kill the waves. I don't think they ever used those, but there were a half a dozen kinds that they used.

Q: The need for all of these things obviously put a strain on industry. Did your outfit have relations with industry?

Quynn: Yes, indirectly. For instance at the Trident conference, we wanted a lot of landing craft. The Army wanted a lot of tanks. The Air Force wanted a lot of airplanes and aircraft carriers. There was only so much metal available.

1 Quynn - 35a

So we had to have these conferences. Of 100 percent metal available, how much would go to landing craft, how much would go to tanks, and how much would go to something else. That's what decided those things. We had many conferences there on those subjects.

Q: This problem of logistics and appreciation of it, it differed somewhat with the British, didn't it? What was their attitude?

Quynn: They weren't confronted with the distances we had. There wasn't any need for these mobile logistic squadrons, because everything that they had was based on England. They just had to get it across the English Channel. That's only a matter of 30 or 40 miles.

Their problem was entirely different from where we had to start it maybe from the west coast and get it two or three thousand miles out in the Pacific. So they never had any problems like we had.

Q: Except when they sent a portion of the Royal Navy out to be a part of the Pacific Fleet. Then they did have a problem.

Quynn: We tied in and we furnished that mostly. They only had a few ships there.

Q: They were geared to land bases.

Quynn: That's right. Of course they were based on Australia, most of them.

Q: Yes, but when they were operating up off Okinawa --

Quynn: We furnished the logistics for all of them. In other words, they were just tied in. They had a couple of carriers, a couple of cruisers, or something like that. They were just a part of our organization.

There again, we would send our own Navy people down to be on the staff of the British Admiral. So they would be part of our Navy really, as far as anything like logistics.

That was another thing in logistics that we had to have. We emphasized that we had to have one head of everything in the way of logistics support. It had to be under one command. In other words the service force Pacific had everything out there, except what was down with MacArthur.

When we got into the Manila thing, we turned what he needed from our outfit over to him. We furnished a logistic squadron down there to take care of his needs, but using our ships and our facilities.

That's what I say, where the coordination was with Admiral Nimitz. A lot of our people went down there and didn't get along with him at all.

Q: You mean, with MacArthur?

Quynn: Yes. Kinkaid was really the first one that got along with him. He was a very smooth person, like Nimitz was. *After the War I was his Chief of Staff for 3½ years when he was Comd. Eastern Sea Frontier*

Q: Was it beneficial for MacArthur to have a separate supply force, separate from the rest?

Quynn: No, it wasn't. We had a lot of trouble with him. I shouldn't discuss these critical things. But for instance - we'd send a ship down there loaded with supplies of some kind, which they had to unload and send back to get some more. He wouldn't send them back. He'd keep them down there.

Q: Keep the ships?

Quynn: Yes.

Q: For what purpose?

Quynn: He had some local supplier that he used. That wasn't part of our plan. Maybe in Australia there were food supplies and things like that that he used those ships for.

In Washington we had a naval transportation service, Coco Smith was head of that at the time. We had control of all of the ships that went into the Pacific, or he did in Washington. I worked with them quite a bit. I know that quite frequently they'd send a ship out, and then never hear from it again.

Q: That must have been irksome.

Quynn: It was, because you couldn't plan accurately, but you tried to plan. You had so many ships, or so many tons, or whatever it was you were going to carry out. When you knew how many ships you had, and an awful lot of them were held out there. They were scheduled, you'd send them out, and expect them back in three or four months or something like that.

Q: Reverting just a moment to the British ships out in the Pacific, they weren't skilled in refueling at sea and that kind of thing, were they?

Quynn: They learned to do it. We weren't either until the war started. That was another one of the problems we had. In order to fuel at sea you've got to get two ships on parallel courses. One ship would have a master gyrocompass and you'd throw a pilot compass over on the other ship. They would both keep the same course. They'd steer a course maybe 20 feet apart. In the early days, they didn't think they could do it. They wanted us to build these large fenders to put over the side of the ship, so if they came together they wouldn't damage the ship. They were sort of awkward and heavy to handle, and never got any place at all. I got into a little difficulty one time, saying the same thing. But actually we never used them anymore. A carrier would fuel from a tanker, with nothing in between them, they just had these gyrocompasses and kept the same courses.

Q: That was really an apt solution, wasn't it?

Quynn: Yes. They did all kinds of things.

With ammunition - take a thousand pound bomb and transfer it from an ammunition ship to a carrier, that's no easy trick either. They made up some kind of a rig (burtoning) a bunch of blocks and tackles whereby you lower away from one ship and haul away on the other ship, and keep a strain on where this bomb is. You eventually get it aboard the carrier without doing any damage. That was something we had to do a lot of experimenting with, but we finally did it. A 16 inch shell is not an easy thing to fool with either.

There were thousands of problems like that. Towards the end of the war, we had them pretty well licked.

The battleships would go in and fire, and when they ran out of ammunition at Kwajalein, Einawetok, or Guam, or someplace when they got through with that, they had to be replenished. They had no place to go, except the Pacific Ocean.

It was remarkable with so many people. Say 2900 ships we had, some of them were in drydock, some were ammunition ships, all kinds of things. We were lucky that we knew where they were.

Q: Admiral, will you talk a little about Admiral Calhoun. He sounds like a genius.

Quynn: He had the same characteristics as Admiral Nimitz in a way, except he didn't spare the horses any when he started talking about the Army aviators - for instance.

He was always talking about them. Admiral Nimitz would say, "You shouldn't do that, Bill. (or whatever he called him) They're trying their best, and they've got to learn."

Actually he didn't work too hard. He had some pretty good people out there, and he turned everything over to them. As long as everything worked, that was all he cared about.

I never did have a big command. I was always Chief of Staff or something like that. I started out with the Assistant Commandant at the Naval Academy. Where I had a lot of control over the midshipmen

Q: Who was the Commandant then?

Quynn: He was Rolston Holmes. He was an outstanding naval officer too, except he had some trouble with his feet. He became an Admiral all right. He was in command of one of the destroyer groups out there. I think he was retired not too long after that. He and Calhoun were good friends. He told Calhoun, "Let me run things for awhile, and see how things go."

Most people, if they get to be top man, don't have to do too much of the detail as long as they have a good staff.

Q: If they've had the wisdom to select a good staff.

Quynn: Of course, that's the main thing. Spruance had a wonderful staff - Charlie Moore, Savvy Forrestal, and two or three other very capable people.

Mick Carney on Halsey's staff was a house afire and got in a little trouble every now and then.

Calhoun was just dedicated to his job. All he wanted was to see Admiral Nimitz, Admiral Halsey — he was a very [Adm Spruance] dear friend of all of them — have anything that they wanted.

Q: You told me before we went on tape, that he once said that to you.

Quynn: We had a lot of problems. For instance — we never knew where some of these ships were going to be. If they wanted to have electronic equipment that they needed, we used to have to send two or three pieces of the same equipment out to different places where we thought these ships might be able to pick them up. That's very uneconomical, but of course war is very uneconomical. Anyway, we were sure they got what they needed.

Towards the end, when they had these Japanese kamikazis, the only defense against them was a smoke screen. We had these things which burned fuel oil, but they burned it inefficiently so they made a lot of smoke. Our ships were around Okinawa, particularly I think. We just had them loaded up with these smoke producers.

One time with Admiral Spruance, we fell a little short. That wasn't so good, but we managed to get them out there a little later.

Q: Admiral Callaghan told me about the early days of the Nimitz staff, and about some communication coming from Washington which upset the Admiral very much. The import was that in joint operations with the Army and so forth there had to be adequate planning in advance for the logistical part of it, and the staff was too small for this. Were you aware of that?

Quynn: Of course I knew him, from way back. He was a very close friend of mine. Before his brother Dan was killed, he and I used to play tennis a lot too. He was out there in the early days, before we even built up very much, on Nimitz's staff. He was his, sort of go between between the service force and Admiral Nimitz's staff.

We had a supply officer out there who was quite a character, Carl Eagle, deceased. He was always trying to find out where things were and what they needed. Callaghan quite frequently went with him. He was the fleet supply officer. He was under me, as Chief of Staff, but he was a very close friend. They called him the 'flying Eagle'. He was pretty good, He was all over, Australia and god knows where, to get everything done.

Later on, the staffs were bigger and everything else. We had more experience, that's the main thing.

One thing about war, you can train and do everything you want in peace time. Until the guns begin to shoot, you've got problems that you couldn't even have anticipated.

Q: Callaghan implied that Admiral Nimitz was somewhat shaken by this communication.

Quynn: I don't remember this particular one. But I do know that the Army often wanted to take care of their own. Their organization was different from ours. In other words, in Washington everything was given to Commander, service force to supply, even the repairs of ships. We had a few arguments there with the Bureau of Ships in Washington too.

We wanted the full authority, because we were in the best position to know what had to be done or where it should be done and so forth. In other words, which naval base out on the west coast could do it, or whether Pearl Harbor could do it, or if it had to go back to Puget Sound, or Mare Island, or something of that kind. We got that finally ironed out.

The Army in the meanwhile, in the early days particularly, wanted to run their own logistics. They had a lot of ships themselves. One of the things that made them unhappy and they were glad to come in to us, we provided better food than the Army did. We went in for what they called 'reefers', frozen things on ships. If you'd go to an island where they'd have a Navy group and an Army group, the Navy group would eat better than the Army group. The naval aviators had the cream of the crop. That was eventually ironed out.

So that when we had an island where you had a garrison. There were some Navy, you always had a naval base. You usually had an Army General in command or sometimes a Marine General. The Navy supplied all the food for all of them. We had control of all of the ships too.

That was one of the things - it was a different organization. In other words, the War Department wanted to deal directly with these groups in outlying places. The Navy would deal with the service force, and we would deal with the groups.

Q: The Navy system was more decentralized.

Quynn: That's right. That didn't last too long, especially when they found out they'd get better food if they dealt with us instead of something else.

Bill Callaghan and I were there. I was there the whole time. He left. He became director of naval transportation. I used to have a lot to do with him out there, and in Washington before that.

Q: In your outfit, the supply service, you enlisted the aid of experts in various areas. Didn't you? How did you go about doing that?

Quynn: The main thing we did was in fuel distribution. As far as everything else went, I think we had people in the Navy; there were a lot of reserves. We had wonderful people there.

There is one thing I was going to tell you about. There was ~~a fellow on~~ an officer our staff who was a lawyer in civil life. He was in the fuel division in one our ourfits there.

We had to bring this fuel, as I told you before, from Aruba out to the Pacific in ~~these~~ bulk carriers. Then we had to discharge them into the fleet carriers, and they would fuel the ships.

He had this schedule made out. It was the darnest thing you've ever seen. It was like a big pipe line starting at Aruba. He had it all sketched out in colors and everything where the bulk carrier would peel off, and where this one would peel off in a smaller pipe line. Then he'd show where they would join up with the fleet carriers, and they would take the fuel in another line wherever their ships were located. I don't say it was 100 percent accurate, but it was a marvelous thing to look at.

Q: It was graphic.

Quynn: You'd just look at it and see what each one was supposed to do - what day, what place, and so forth. It was a terrific job. He was interested in that kind of work, and that's what he did. You had to know a couple of months ahead of time actually where each tanker of fuel was going. It was very interesting to see what was going to happen.

Q: Tell me about Admiral Nimitz's sense of humor, as you experienced it.

Quynn: All I know is that at these conferences we had he usually came up with some little joke, not an off color joke, but one that fitted in with the situation or something of that kind.

When you were with him playing tennis or horseshoes, he had these little stories to tell.

He was very canny, that is the word that a lot of people use to describe him. I don't know whether he was Scotch or not.

Q: He was German actually.

Quynn: Yes, I guess he was, sure.

That term has been used in numerous write ups that I've seen in the paper from time to time.

In other words, he didn't commit himself in any way to cause friction or get into trouble with the other services or anything like that. He didn't do that.

There were a lot of times, I know from certain sources, that he didn't approve of what was being done. Instead of bawling somebody out, he would get the word to them in a genteel way and the same result was accomplished.

Q: It has been said about him, his son told me that it applied to him too, that the Admiral established in various ways certain standards. His expectations was that those who worked with him would meet those standards. He never outlined them but he merely expected it and you complied.

Quynn: I'm afraid I can't answer that question very well, because I wasn't directly on his staff. Most of the time I saw him was at tennis or horseshoes or a couple of times over there at dinner with him.

I never heard any member of his staff say that. I know he got along very well with everybody on the staff. They thought he was a wonderful man, and he was.

He wasn't Halsey type, and neither was Spruance. He was sort of a little shy, you might say.

He never sought publicity. Both Spruance and Nimitz were criticised for that because when they really had done things, they thought the public ought to know about it. But they wouldn't open their mouths very much to newspaper correspondents or war correspondents.

Q: That was pretty much in the Navy tradition anyway, wasn't it?

Quynn: Yes it was. Except Halsey got an awful lot of publicity, and he did get some criticism. He should have gotten some criticism for that typhoon business. Those things are hard to handle.

Out in China, we had typhoons on the scope all the time. You never knew when you went to sea if you were going to run into a typhoon or not.

I got caught in one. I'm surprised we didn't sink, but we did hold on. This was out of Hong Kong. It wasn't supposed to hit Hong Kong, but it turned around and did at 164 miles an hour. It put 27 ships on the beach in Hong Kong harbor.

They're very careful out there. They report these typhoons — what intensity they're going to be and when they're going to hit and so forth. All the ships in the harbor would adjust their moorings and locations to meet them.

They didn't get the word on this. I've got the picture in here of 10,000 ton ships right up on the front street in Hong Kong.

Hong Kong harbor is well protected in a way, but it's just like a funnel. There're fairly big mountains all around it. The wind just goes right down in there.

INDEX

for an interview

with

REAR ADMIRAL ALLEN G. QUYNN, U. S. NAVY (RETIRED)

Air Force, 35

Argonne, 4, 17

Army, 13, 29-30, 32, 34-35, 44-45; aviators, 40

Bogue, Como. Jimmie, 27

Calhoun, Admiral William L., 2, 40-42

California, 22

Callaghan, VADM William M., 43-45

Carney, Robert B., Adm. 25, 41

Churchill, Winston, 34

Davis, Admiral Arthur C., 6-7, 11

Eagle, Carl, 43

Einawetok, 14, 33, 40

Eisenhower, President Dwight, 30-31

Ford Island, 17

Forrestal, Admiral Emmet Peter, 41

Guam, 5, 20, 23-24, 32, 46

Halsey, Admiral William Frederick, 22, 41-42, 48-49

Holmes, Rolston, 41

Hong Kong, 49-50

Kimmel, Husband A., 1, 4, 21

Kimmel, Mrs. Husband E., 21

King, Admiral Ernest J., 34

Kinkaid, Admiral Thomas C., 37

Kushua Island, 4

Kwajalein, 14, 33, 40

MacArthur, General Douglas, 28-29, 36-38

Manila, 36

Marine Corps, 13, 29, 32, 45

McCormick, Admiral Lynn, 11

McMorris, Admiral Charles H., 29

Midway, Battle of, 1, 6-9, 11

Moore, RADM Charles J., 41

Naval Academy, 31

Naval Aviators, 29, 44

New Jersey, 14

Nimitz, Mrs. Chester W., 21

Okinawa, 15-16, 20, 42

Pearl Harbor, 2-4, 6-8, 14-15, 18, 21; Day, 16-17, 21-22, 44

Pennsylvania, 4

Roosevelt, President F. D., 34

Saipan, 20

Seabees, 23-25

Service Force, 3-6, 23-25, 28, 37-38, 45-46

Sherman, Admiral Forest, 6, 26

Smith, General Holland, 31-32

Smith, Senator Margaret Chase, 12

Smith, William Ward, 38

Spruance, Admiral Raymond Ames, 8, 10, 13-14, 32, 41-42, 48

Steele, Captain James M., 9, 11, 17

Tarawa, 19

Towers, Admiral John, 5, 20

Trident Conference, 34-35a

Truk, 26

Utah, 17

Vireo, 8, 11

Waunamee, 26

West Point, 31

Yorktown, 8, 11

DECLARATION OF TRUST

The undersigned does hereby appoint and designate as his (her) Trustee herein, the Secretary-Treasurer and Publisher of the United States Naval Institute to perform and discharge the following duties, powers, and privileges in connection with the possession and use of a certain taped interview between the undersigned and the Oral History Department of the United States Naval Institute.

(1) As an <u>Open</u> transcript it may be read (or the tape audited) by qualified researchers upon presentation of proper credentials as determined by the Trustee. In the case of interviews about the late Fleet Admiral C. W. Nimitz, it is intended that first use of the material shall be made by the biographer of the Fleet Admiral, Professor E. B. Potter, and the Naval Institute is authorized to deal with the material in this fashion.

(2) It is expressly understood that in giving this authorization, I am in no way precluded from placing such restrictions as I may desire upon use of the interview at any time during my lifetime, nor does this authorization in any way affect my rights to the copyright of any literary expressions that may be contained in the interview.

Witness my hand and seal this 13th day of January 1970.

John H. Redman

I hereby accept and consent to the foregoing Declaration of Trust and the powers therein conferred upon me as Trustee:

R. E. Bowker
Secretary-Treasurer and Publisher

Vice Admiral John R. Redman　　　　　　by John T. Mason, Jr.
Subject: Admiral Nimitz　　　　　　　　June 5, 1969

Mr. Mason: Admiral, it's awfully good of you to see me today and to talk about your relations with Fleet Admiral Nimitz. As you know, we at the Naval Institute, are attempting to gather a great deal of information on the Admiral in anticipation of a biography of him. Although there is so very very much in the Navy Department on his official career; there isn't much on Nimitz, the man. It is from his personal friends and family, that we can obtain this kind of information. Since you were a close friend, of his, I came to you, and I hope today you will tell me something about your relations with him. Would you begin perhaps Admiral, by telling me how you first met him, when you first met, and things of that sort?

Admiral Redman: I had known of Admiral Nimitz and his reputation for some years, when I was a young officer. My first opportunity to meet him came about through some circumstances that took place right here in San Francisco when I was a young officer.

　　I was Inspector Instructor of the Communications Volunteer Reserve here in San Francisco. The leader of that group was a man of German extraction. He was a very capable x-ray man.

Redman - 2

Q: What time was this, what date?

Redman: This was between 1927-29, when I performed that duty here. It seems that later on in the beginning of World War II, he came under suspicion because he was rather vocal about the performances of the Germans in Europe - this was before we got into the war. Somebody took some spite out on him, and sicked the F.B.I. onto him. They were about to eliminate him from his Naval Reserve status - I think he was a Lieutenant Commander at that time. I knew the man very well, and he wrote to me that he was in trouble. I got ahold of this F.B.I. report.

Q: Where were you then, in Washington?

Redman: I was in Washington by that time. I got ahold of this F.B.I. report and read it. My judgement was that it was a silly performance. This young F.B.I. fellow had reported such things as -- wearing a part of a navy uniform - it turned out to be a khaki shirt- at a picnic. And that he'd been heard to say that the Germans were licking the hell out of the British.

Q: Indeed they were, weren't they?

Redman: They were at that time. I was so incensed about this, and I couldn't get any place with the particular officer who was in charge of that subject in the Bureau of Personnel - Bureau of Navigation it was at that time, I think. I asked for an audience with Admiral Nimitz.

Q: He was then the Head of BuNav?

Redman: He was Chief of the Bureau at that time. He was placed in this position of possibly overiding this decision of one of his subordinates. I explained this whole thing to him, and I gained the impression at that time of what a wonderful understanding man he was. He gave me assurance that he would give this thing his attention. It ended up by - rather than placing the officer in question in an embarrassing position in regard to his future, they gave him an honorary reserve retirement. Which pleased us. He was an elder at that time, at any rate.

I was very impressed with Admiral Nimitz's sympathy, and his decision in this case because he didn't want to override a Captain under him in the Bureau.

I never saw him again, or had any contact with him until later on in World War II. I was ordered to his staff as Pacific Fleet Communications Officer.

Q: About when was this sir?

Redman - 4

Redman: This was in 1942. September or October 1942 I reported to his Staff. I had been up to that time in charge of the Radio Intelligence section of the Office of Chief of Naval Operations. I had quite a little bit to do with the question of the utilization of our efforts in connection with the Japanese codes, ciphers, The Battle of Midway, and all that.

When I was ordered out to his staff, he received me very nicely. I reported just after one of the battles in the South Pacific when we'd lost a carrier there. I think, at that time we were down to one carrier in active commission, and another that was being repaired. He had reason to be depressed. I again looked upon him as a man who rose above everything. He greeted me, and gave me encouragement. He said, "Now we've got a job to do. We've got one carrier left. Let's get at it."

Q: Were you replacing one of Kimmel's staff people?

Redman: I replaced Commander M. E. Curts, and he in turn was ordered to Admiral King's staff in the Department. I was sent out to relieve him. I was offered to Admiral Nimitz as a replacement for Curts and was accepted by Admiral Nimitz.

This was at the time when the tide was turning in the South Pacific, and we had a great deal of work to do. We were in - we called it the dug out - headquarters that was built there at Pearl Harbor after the attack.

One other reason why I had some personal contact with him was because at the time that they built the headquarters there - the bomb proof headquarters, they called it - they still weren't too sure that the Japs might not come in there and bomb the place. They established the idea of a secondary emergency headquarters in one house in the officers quarters. One of the quarters was set up as a secondary communications center.

Q: That was quite a thing to do, wasn't it? To have a secondary one, with all the equipment.

Redman: Yes, it was enough equipment to operate with in case Admiral Nimitz's quarters - the bomb proof headquarters - should be bombed, and put out of commission. In this house, there were generators on the back porch. There were safes with the code books in them. There were places for operating the machines. There was an operation room.

Q: It was a kind of a duplicate of the headquarters.

Redman: Very very minor, small affair. As Fleet Communications Officer I was allowed to live in these quarters. There were extra bedrooms upstairs. It was a good idea to have somebody live there. I had my radio officer with me, and another Captain who was in charge of the Intelligence Activities came along later. The three of us lived there together. Because this was a beautiful set of quarters, we always kept it a secret as to what was in the building. Every once in a while, one of the subordinate Admirals to Admiral Nimitz around there would say, "Admiral why have you got those three Captains living in that beautiful house up there? Why isn't that made available to some Flag Officer?"

Admiral Nimitz would write me a note and say, "Redman, I'll entertain a recommendation from you as to whether you and these other two Captains should continue to live there. Maybe you still need that thing." I recommended that we continue the arrangement a few times, but eventually we felt we should move out. That was only a few months before we moved out to Guam. W lasted there for quite a while.

Q: But you still maintained the equipment there?

Redman: Oh, yes. It was still a possibility. Of course, the Japs were getting further and further away by that time. In between these quarters and the Admiral's quarters was a horseshoe pit. The Admiral used to love to pitch horseshoes. Every once in a while he'd send over for somebody, and get one of us like a fourth for Bridge, to come and pitch horseshoes. We used to see a lot of him that way.

Q: Did you get involved in those afternoons of exercise, too, on the beach?

Redman: Oh, yes, I'll have to tell you about that. He and Admiral Spruance were the healthiest people on the staff, I think. We'd all be busy down there at our desks in the headquarters, and the word would go around like lightning that the Admiral and the Chief of Staff were planning to go over to Kailua across the Island. That meant going over to this beach on the far side of the Island, and walking down the beach about four or five miles at a very brisk pace, and walking out into the ocean and beginning to swim back. They never swam all the way back, but sometimes the two Admirals - Admiral Nimitz and his Chief of Staff - would swim back about a mile or a mile and a half. They used to kill the rest of us.

Q: What kind of libation or refreshment did you get when you got back?

Redman: From them?

Q: Yes.

Redman: Oh, nothing. They turned us loose, we went home to our own quarters, and got our own libation. When the word would go around the corner that the Chief of Staff and the

Redman - 8

Admiral were getting ready for a hike over to Kaulua, everybody would go under their desk or hide in the closet.

Q: Previous engagement?

Redman: The Marines would go around to everybody's office saying that Admiral Nimitz and Admiral Spruance wanted to know if there were any volunteers who wanted to go over to Kaulua. That was funny.

Q: Did they know how popular their exercise period was?

Redman: I don't think they did, but they might have counted noses every once in a while. They were a little bit surprised that they didn't get the same people too often. They only wanted about five or six, in addition to themselves.

Q: Was there any time for just social conversation on an expedition like that -- or was it all ??

Redman: Yes, the Admiral would take one or two under his wing, and have a chat with them, and things like that. I went a couple of times, but I wasn't in as good a condition as they were. They were in excellent physical condition. It was really surprising. I think it was a wonderful thing that they did that. I played tennis; I was a golfer before I went out there.

They had a very nice set-up there at the Headquarters. They had about five or six tennis courts right in the area where the quarters were. It was a very compact arrangement. We lived a seven day week, and there was no time to go play a game of golf, because you just couldn't be that far away from your desk. But both Chiefs of Staff - I went through two Chiefs of Staff, Admiral Spruance and then Admiral McMorris who followed him - were both very considerate about the officers. If you went to either Chief of Staff, and said, "I'm going up to the tennis court to play a little tennis." They'd say, "Fine, I know where you are."

I was called upon quite often because of communication problems.

Q: Yes, you had to be like a doctor, didn't you? Including, at night, and any other time?

Redman: Yes. I lived next door to the Admiral. Of course, we spent an awful lot of office hours down there.

With regard to the tennis courts, we'd go up there and play tennis. The Chief of Staff would make it easy on you, try not to pull you back to the headquarters if he could. He'd send up an orderly or somebody with a question. You could write on a pad and send the answer back. Of course if it needed your presence, you'd abandon your game and go on back down.

Q: You certainly had to have a bit of levity.

Redman: Oh, they were that. Both Admiral Nimitz and Admiral Spruance were very much in favor of exercise to keep you in physical condition. I think it was a very wise thing.

I've forgotten what the size of that staff was out there. I have a picture some place. In my own case, I had about 130 to 140 Ensigns and J.G.s working for me and about 35 more senior officers on a planning staff.

Another thing that the Admiral liked to do in the way of exercise -- most of my activities were down in the basement, down in the bomb proof shelter. You've never been in that place?

Q: No, I haven't.

Redman: I had all of these rooms down there, and these officers working. On the planning staff, we did our own planning for establishing new radio stations, and things of that kind. I had quite a number of radio engineer officers. And a major assistant who was a radio officer. I wasn't a number one radio engineer, I was more on the side of communications. I had about 35 people in the planning and engineering side of radio communications. In communications - the Navy Department and the Admiral counted on us to do our own job. Which was not only communications, but it was creating new radio stations. And setting up new radio networks, providing the frequencies for them and the operations and equipment. So we had our own personnel officer. We handled all our assignments of officers to these sources - not so much the ships. The Bureau of Personnel took pretty good care of the ships. With regard to these islands we were taking back from the Japanese, it was like establishing new territory.

Q: Did you have to be in direct contact then with the Commander of the operation of that island?

Redman: Oh, yes. That which I just cited was one of the reasons that I had the privilege of being in close contact with the Admiral on several occasions. The fact that when the Marines would re-take an island - like Guadalcanal, or Tarawa or Kwajalein or Mariannas - the Admiral would be very anxious as quickly as possible to fly into these places, and have a look. As a matter of fact, he was fearless with regard to his own safety - too much so. The Chief of Staff would worry and try to keep him at home for as long as he could. The Admiral would want to get in there too soon.

Q: Admiral Nimitz was something of a fatalist, wasn't he?

Redman: Yes, he was, that's right. Because of this communication organization in these islands, and the Admiral would want to fly in there and see one of them; he would take me along because I'd told him about my problems. I had to set up a radio station, and get communications going, and put them in a network. The first thing ashore after the Marines, was a portable communication station.

Q: Yes, that made sense.

Redman:
The Admiral would take me, and he'd take the doctor. He always took his Fleet Doctor along. He had two wonderful doctors - the first one was Jondreau, who was killed; and the second one was Anderson; as I recall. He'd take the doctors and he'd take me, and fly into these places and have a look. And I'd play Cribbage with him to and from; we played Cribbage all the time in the plane.

Sighting his fearlessness and disregard for his own safety - I remember that when we went into Tarawa, and we looked at Tarawa, we had to fly around in the air for awhile. We went down to some smaller island below Tarawa, and then got into a Marine combat paratroop plane, Then we went up to Tarawa, and they were still trying to clean up the island and bulldoze the airstrip. We flew around for nearly an hour before they would let us land. They were trying to make something out of this airstrip so that we could land on it. Here was the Admiral in this Marine paratroop plane. We landed there, and we walked around the island taking a look at everything.

That was the first place where the Marines learned that you just can't take dead enemy bodies and bulldoze earth over them, or coral or whatever was available. In those hot climates, magots would appear in short order and rise to the surface. That was the status that the place was in, too hurriedly bulldozed over.

Q: So they had to dig trenches in those islands.

Redman: Yes. In Kwajalein, later on, they learned that they had to dig down deep, and they had to treat them with chemicals, put a layer over them, and more chemicals, and so forth. So they finally got them down so that nothing ever rose to the surface again.

Q: Wasn't there also the danger of booby traps, and grenades, and things? Or was it too late for that?

Redman: That existed in any event. What I'm talking about is the question of disposal of dead bodies, and things like that.

In Tarawa, there was a Japanese seven-inch gun - the MARYLAND, as I recall the name of one of the old battleships - had made a direct hit on this concrete emplacement of this seven-inch gun. It had an enormous basement underground to it that contained ammunition. The side had been knocked out of that. As we walked around the island, we looked in there. Of course, a terrific fire had taken place with this ammunition that blew up - there were about 14 or 16 dead Japanese in there. The Admiral and all the rest of us peeked in there, and looked at these people, and kind of wondered about warfare -- so to speak.

Do you know, when we went back to Pearl Harbor, we heard about a week to ten days later a Japanese who was dying of thirst, a fanatic; came out of that emplacement - out of that very area firing a machine gun. He was shot by the Marines because he was running amuck. Here the Admiral had been peering in there, and that fellow was probably hiding down there.

Q: Was it really necessary for him to take those risks? Was it necessary for him to be on the spot so quickly?

Redman: No, it was his own interest in what was going on. Those were the kinds of things that bothered the Chief of Staff. He always wanted to jump in a plane and go see. He wanted to look at these things himself.

Q: He was the boss, so nobody could restrain him.

Redman: That's right. To get back to this athletic business -- I remember down in the basement of the headquarters, he would bring people down and show them around once in awhile. The Communications Center down in the basement was one of the things to see, of course. He was down there one day, and something came up about bowling. I think I brought it up. He asked me where I was the afternoon before;;he said he'd been looking for me.

I said I went up to the Aiea, the Naval Hospital above the headquarters there. (We eventually lost that hospital to one of the government civilian organizations - Public Health I guess.) In fact, it was a temporary naval hospital that had been established. They had five beautiful brand new bowling alleys.

I discovered it because I had some dental problems and I got acquainted with the dental officer up there; and learned about the bowling alley. I used to go up there and bowl once in awhile.

I told the Admiral where I was the day before, and he said, "I didn't know there were any bowling alleys up there." I said, "Yes, there're some beautiful alleys, Admiral." "Look", he said, "I bowled 230 up in Bremerton one time. I tell you what you do. We'll have five-man teams. You get some youngster that can bowl pretty good. You and I will challenge the doctors up there to a five-man team match. We'll go up there once in awhile and we'll bowl them for the coca-colas."

So, I called up the Commanding Officer of the hospital, and told him the Admiral's idea, and he said, "Great, just call anytime you want. We'll get together a team."

Every once in awhile I'd go up to the Admiral - it was only about 15 minutes striking distance to come back to his headquarters, in the utilities where he was - and say, "Things are kind of quiet, Admiral. Would you like to go bowl this afternoon?" He'd look at his desk, at the paper work on it and so forth; and he's aay, "Yes, line it up." So, we'd go and bowl three rounds, and the losing team paid for the coca-colas, He just loved it. That gave him another out, to get some exercise.

Q: He'd always been a bowler, I guess.

Redman: Yes, he was a pretty good bowler too.

Q: Mrs. Nimitz tells me that she bowled with him earlier in their married life.

Redman: I've forgotten how old the Admiral was when he was CinCPac Fleet, and CinCPoa. I think the high bracket that he bowled at that time was 215. That's pretty good bowling, you know.

Redman - 17

Q: He hadn't been doing it at all?

Redman: No, he hadn't been doing it for some time. This experience that he talked about would have been up in Bremerton when he was much younger.

Q: Tell me about the staff meetings that you had.

Redman: It was the custom - Sundays didn't mean anything on the staff, at the headquarters - every day was alike. I can remember when you'd get so tired of this routine that you'd say, "This is February, if somebody would tell me that next October 15th that I could sleep in; I'd have something to look forward to." That's the way it was, because we were down there early in the morning, every day, seven days a week. Unless you were off on a trip, or something like that.

He had a staff meeting every single morning when things were normal there. It consisted of all of the major members of the staff. The usual procedure was for one of the officers to brief the staff on intelligence that had come in in the last 24 hours. Then there would be a discussion on any planned operations, future operations. Or, if there'd been some kind of an event afloat in the Pacific sometime previously and the survivors were beginning to arrive back - they usually funneled through Pearl Harbor on their back to the coast -

chosen people who had gone through some particular experience would be asked to address the staff. So, it was always very interesting every morning, because you never knew just what you were going to hear about, or perhaps see new faces and new people coming through. That, in general, was it.

Then, he might dismiss everybody except maybe two or three people that he wanted to talk to about something special.

I was usually allowed to listen to practically everything because the Admiral knew that --

Q: You saw all the dispatches anyway?

Redman: I saw all the dispatches anyway, and that I had to plan. I had a planning problem of my own, in addition to the planning problem of the operations group. If they were going to go here or there, or if they were going to take an island, or some kind of an afloat operation -- I had the problem of communications, and I had the problem of radio frequencies, and the problem of operators and asking Washington for radio equipment. That not only involved the Navy, but it involved the Pacific Ocean area, and all the other forces.

I can recall - for instance -- General Richardson was the leading Army man in Oahu at that time. The Air Corps hadn't gained their autonomy at that place at that time. Every once in awhile the Admiral would send for me, and I'd be - you might say, up on the carpet - because I'd issued some kind of a directive that either the Army or the Air Corps felt didn't respect their autonomy. I remember twice this happened. The Admiral sent for me, and he said, "Redman, (he never called me Jack until after we retired, always the last name) --

Q: That was pretty much his habit anyway.

Redman: Oh, yes, that's usually a military habit.

Q: In letters he wrote, I have seen this always, he addresses by the last name.

Redman: Around here, in the years before he died; when I was a Commandant and I was his logistical support, you might say, he changed it and called me by my first name.

At that time, he said, "Redman, General Richardson has complained that you are interfering with the Army's communications, by such and such a directive you put out." Of course, I'd take these directives to him. Which was a rather expansive deal because it involved the use of codes and ciphers, the use of radio frequencies, the use of personnel, allocation of personnel. Which was limited, we weren't training people fast enough. We had a big expansion deal going on out there in the Pacific. Somebody had to lay the law down, you see. We would pinch here and there, but I was the one who had to spread the frequencies and spread the personnel.

Q: He was CinC, and --

Redman: And responsibility. Another thing was a question of overloading the circuits, too. Carelessness and freedom of   and messages-- too long-winded in what you wanted to say. Brevity was essential in order to keep it down, so that the traffic would flow and the important message wouldn't be lost behind something where somebody talked too much -- those kind of things.

I'd sit there, and the Admiral would tell me what General Richardson had complained about. I'd go all through just what I've been telling you about. About the problems I was faced with, and the necessity for this directive. Maybe some Air Force outfit had complained to General Richardson. Of course, he had to go and represent them to Admiral Nimitz.

After I'd get through, the Admiral would say, "General, you heard him. Don't you think we ought to give him another chance?" The General would say, "We have to, we don't understand it." He was great.

Q: Were you there at the time of the Ghormley incident?

Redman: Yes, I was. You mean when the decision was made to relieve Admiral Ghormley?

Q: Yes.

Redman: I was very very fond of Admiral Ghormley. I knew more about that then a lot of people did. I was on duty in Washington when Admiral Ghormley came back from London. I saw that Admiral Ghormley was only given a very brief period of time to get prepared, and to put a staff together. No Admiral is self-sufficient, he's got to have a good staff. He had a very very short time in Washington after he came back from London. I've forgotten what his job was in London.

Q: I think he was a Naval Attache, wasn't he?

Redman: Could have been, I'm not sure. I think he was a Rear Admiral over there. They made him a Vice Admiral and sent him out to the Pacific.

Just as an example - of course, I was only a Communicator, and I was closest to the Communications side of the thing. I'll just put this in here as 'off the record' -- It's hardly fair to say something that discredits the capabilities of a particular officer, because this could be re- searched. They gave him as a Communications Officers - a youngster whose only experience was a code-room Officer in the Navy Department, as his Communications Officer. Commander South Pacific was the job. They gave him a wonderful Chief of Staff - Dan Callahan, he was the greatest. Couldn't have done better by him than Dan Callahan as Chief of Staff. He had to throw this staff together very hurriedly, and go down there to the South Pacific.

I'm only a Communicator. I'm not a logistic man or not an operational man - that is as far as the Pacific is concerned - but this is just my viewpoint of the thing. He went down to the South. Admiral Ghormley tried to line up what he thought was the proper situation in regard to what he had to do. That involved the unloading of ships. He picked out Aukland to handle the unloading of these ships, even though the action was way up in the Solomon's; with Guadalcanal the first objective to take. He was told, rather abruptly I'd say, to get up near the front. So, he had to go to Noumea. Noumea had only one dock. They didn't have harbor space for the unloading of the ships. The loading of the ships wasn't the best, from the point of view of logistical overseeing here in the United States when they loaded the ships. There'd be seven crates in the bottom of the hole in one ship, and the important center of the whole assembly was in another ship. It meant unloading these ships, and trying to sort this stuff out. He had to have room, he had to lay it out and put it together, and so forth. Aukland was the only place, and that was the logical place. They had a beautiful docks and everything, even though it was an extra thousand miles to the South - or about 800. With the time that it took ships to travel -- after they put this stuff together and got it ready to use -- that time was insignificant compared to the time taken to do it in a place where you didn't have any room to do it in. He had no room to unload, and then he had to try and do it by

Things didn't go so well. Admiral Nimitz had a staff meeting. --- How did you know about that?

Q: He told me himself.

Redman: He did? He had a staff meeting at the time, and I sat there and listened. When he got down through the staff, he said, "Redman, what about your affairs? What do you recommend?" I said, "Admiral, I'm going to only treat it from my point of view - my line of business, so to speak. Admiral Ghormley doesn't have a very good Communication Officer. Admiral Halsey has got an excellent Communication Officer." That's all I said. That may or may not have to contributed to the ultimate decision. I hated to have to say something because I loved Admiral Ghormley. I thought he was a great guy; I hated to see him relieved. I don't think he got a fair shake out of the whole deal down there. He came back and they made him Com.14. I used to go over and see him once in awhile.

The 14th Naval District is the Hawaiian area. I'd known him in Washington or Annapolis, or some place before. We were pretty good friends. I used to go over and chat with him quite often. I always remember - he called me Jack. I'd tell him a lot of the things that were going on. I'd tell him a lot of things that I thought were wrong, too. He was a great guy. He never was bitter at all about having been pulled out of the South Pacific, and made Com.14. He said, "Jack, you know the trouble with you?" I said, "No, what's that?" He said, "You look under too many beds."

Q: Find skeletons.

Redman: The Admiral was originally a pretty good tennis player, but he didn't indulge in tennis very much. I think he played two or three times.

Q: That's normally reserved for a younger man, isn't it?

Redman: Yes, but he was in good physical shape when he was out there.

Q: Tell me about his seemingly great ability to keep a level head and not to get upset by a bad turn of events, that kind of thing.

Redman: Oh, yes, that's where he excelled. It was his basic character. He never never got excited. He was very calm, but he could always make a decision - even though it hurt. I never saw him get worked up to any degree about anything.

I was going to tell you another anecdote about him.

Q: Fine, do.

Redman: I mentioned that he and I used to play Cribbage in the plane. To go back -- the first flight that I ever made with him was shortly after I reported out there, but this time we didn't fly alone. This time he wanted to go down and look into the Guadalcanal area. So, we flew down in a big seaplane - it was a four-engine seaplane - the type I can't recall. We landed at Espiritu Santo.

Q: It probably was a Sunderland flying boat, wasn't it?

Redman: No, the Navy didn't operate any Sunderlands.

Q: Catalina?

Redman: It was a four-engine flying boat.

He wanted to go down with the staff and take a look at Guadalcanal. We had a three-star Admiral - his first name was Jake - he was in charge of all the air operations -- all of the Navy and Army Air Corps operations down in that area.

Q: That wasn't Hoover?

Redman: No, it wasn't Hoover.

We stopped at Espiritu Santo and he gave us a B-17, because there were no water landings for a seaplane up at Guadalcanal. That is, there were no water landings that we could trust; because the Japs would have picked us off, if we had attempted to go into their lagoons. So, we had to land on the air strip. The air strip at that time was about 2,000 feet of metal matting, and about 1,000 feet of dirt which was full of 100 pound bomb craters which had been patched up.

We all went up in one B-17. We spent two days with General Vandergrift. The Japanese were all around us at that time, all around the air strip, everywhere. We spent a couple of days in there watching the operations. They didn't bombard at that time. But they had been bombarding the air strip with naval gunfire, and bombing --

Q: They were pretty close.

Redman: They were close, and they were all over the island, too.

That was the first time I had heart of palm to eat. It wasn't heart of palm salad. They had great big flat pancake size slices.

Q: Made from the heart of palm?

Redman: From the heart of palm. They knocked down more heart of palm on that island than you can shake a stick at.

Two days later, after we got in there, we were to leave. We got down on the air strip. They decided because of the load, they couldn't land with the load of his staff and himself. It wasn't his entire staff - I think he had about ten of us there with him. So, he decided to divide it up in two loads when we took off. The Admiral was going to take off in the first plane.

Q: A fuel problem, it must have been.

Redman: No, to lighten the plane to get off of the short air strip.

The Admiral, typical of him, got up in the bombardier's area in the nose - this plexiglass forward area of the plane.

This pilot - I had talked to him before - only had one piece of clothing on which was a zipper-coverall and bare feet. Of course it was hot down there, you couldn't blame him. And a black beard. He was a Major in the Army Air Corps. He was the pilot of this B-17.

Q: Sounds like one of the original hippies.

Redman: Exactly. The Admiral gets up in the nose of the plane, and he takes two or three of his staff with him. I could have gone with the Admiral, but after seeing this hippie - so to speak - I decided I'd wait for the second plane. I'll tell you what happened to me later.

The Admiral says to him, "How are you going to take off?" He says, "Admiral, I thought because the field matting is up at this end, even though it's downwind; I can get up to flying speed easy here on the metal matting. I'll probably be up to flying speed before I reach that dirt section." The Admiral said, "All right." He climbed in the plane, and got up in the nose. That's where he wanted to ride, he wanted to see what was going on. So, this Major gets up there, and he guns the thing for all it's worth. He takes off down the strip, and gets just about to the end of the metal matting - which is the first 2,000 feet - and he decides he can't make it.

So, then he cuts all of his engines, and tries to break the thing. He hadn't left the ground. He did a horizontal loop at the end of the field with the tail hanging over the end of the field, and it was a canyon down there. There was a deep canyon at the end of this runway.

The Admiral's sitting up in the nose. We all just -- our hearts were in our throats. He was turned around in the opposite direction when he finally came to a stop. He didn't have another 15 feet to go before he'd have fallen into this canyon. He taxies back up the field. The Admiral gets out of the plane and he said, "Let's all go up to the General's house and have lunch. We'll try this again after lunch." That's all he said.

Q: After reflection, we'll try it again.

Redman: So, we all went up and had a little lunch, and then came back down. Of course, this was wasting time, and that wasn't good. The time to get into Espiritu Santo, was to get in there before dark because they had no lighting on the air field at Espiritu Santo.

So, he got down there again. The Admiral gets in the same plane, the same pilot. This time, because there was a little breeze from the opposite end; they backed the plane clear up to the canyon, he started on the dirt, got onto the matting, and got it into the air all right.

We followed him by about 20 minutes in another B-17. We got about two-thirds or three-quarters of the way down to Espiritu and word trickled through the plane that we couldn't find Espiritu Santo. We were lost; it was getting dark. We were in the radio shack and in the shack there was a great big 100 gallon tank for extra fuel.

To go back -- a classmate of mine - Dan Callaghan's brother - Vice Admiral Bill Callaghan -- he's a great person too. He's one of the people you ought to interview sometime. He was on the staff. William M. Callaghan lives in Washington -- he's handy to you.

So, Bill and I were in this radio shack leaning on this big tank. We saw this engineer come in --

Q: To examine the tank?

Redman: He came in and looked all around the tank, and went out again. Then he came in and scratched his head and took the top off the tank. Bill and I were leaning there. Here was the gasoline shimmying about a half inch from the top of the tank where he took off this cap. It was about three inches in diameter. He kind of nodded; he thought there ought to be gasoline in there. When he took the cap off, one of the radiomen was sitting on the deck smoking a cigarette. I kicked him gently, and told him very quietly to put out the cigarette.

The engineer went back into the next compartment. He comes back out and scratched his head again. Bill and I kind of looked at each other. We knew he was looking for gasoline. He was looking to hook up some gasoline from this tank. He'd go in there, and he'd twist valves, and nothing would happen. He came in to us, and he said, "Let me know if the gasoline goes down." So, Bill and I watched the gasoline. Bill and I would shake our heads, we'd say, "No, it wasn't going down." He'd scratch his head, and he twisted some more knobs. Finally he came, went around behind the tank, and he came out with the end of the hose. Then he looked real bright. He took the hose through the doorway and hooked it on to something in the other compartment. Finally he came back, and said to us, "You know, they forgot to connect it up." It was about that time we discovered we were lost. And it was getting dark.

Another officer of the staff - he's gone now, you won't be able to talk to him - he was another classmate, he was the Fleet Aviator.

Bill Callaghan was the Fuel Oil man, and the Shipping man - Logistics. He had a great deal to do with the moving of fuel oil, tankers, merchant shipping, and those kind of things. Subsequently, he was one of the early - if not the first - heads of the MSTS Department, under the Navy. Wonderful guy, you shouldn't miss him.

Q: I made a note on him.

Redman - 32

Redman: Vice Admiral William M. Callaghan, retired. He lives on Runnymede Street in the District.

To get back to the B-17 --

Q: Yes, you're leaving me in the air here, in suspense.

Redman: After this instance about connecting up the gas tank, we breathed a sigh of relief, that they were able to hook up this extra gasoline. We kept listening for a motor to begin to cough, but none did. Then we got word that we were lost.

Q: Was the first plane lost too?

Redman: No, but we didn't know anything about them at the time. It began to get dark. The navigator finally said, "I don't know where I am." Everybody was looking for Espiritu Santo on the starboard bow of the plane. They were all looking in that direction. It was getting dark.

Q: You needed a 'Captain Weems' on board for star nivagation.

Redman: We sure did. The other classmate that was on there was Ralph Ofstie - he was the Fleet Aviator. He passed away not long ago, I think he was a Vice Admiral on the active list. He died of cancer.

He had taken the precaution - in view of this flying trip down there - to pick up a chart. Being a good Naval Officer, he said he thought he'd take a chart along. If it hadn't been for him and that chart, and his figuring that we must be drifting to the right or something like that; and his taking a look out of one of the portholes in the plane, to the left - nobody would have seen a slender thread of something in the sky. It was almost complete darkness by that time. Gas beginning to be a question, we'd have just plunked into the Pacific, and nobody would have ever found out what happened to us. He looked over there and he saw this thread; and he called it to the attention of the pilot. He said, "I think that probably is a searchlight over there."

So, we flew in that direction, and it was a searchlight. What had happened was that the Admiral had gotten in there in the daylight in the first plane, in the first B-17. He anxiously waited for us. He had several important members of his staff still out there that he was worried about.

He told this Vice Admiral 'Jake', "You tell the CURTIS to put her biggest searchlight up in the air, straight up in the air." That was a seaplane tender that was anchored in the harbor there. Of course, they were darkening ships in those days. He didn't care about any possible attack by the Japs. He was going to get his staff back, or else.

Q: That was priority.

Redman: That was priority. That was the needle that we saw when we turned and went over there. The Admiral's plane had gotten in all right in the daylight. They very hurriedly put some gasoline drums, filled them with waste covered with oil up and down this air strip; and lit them. We used these burning drums as a guide, and we hit the strip all right, and got in there. That was quite an experience.

Q: It's almost a story like that of General Nate Twining, when he told me his story. They did come on down in the Pacific. They were lost for, I don't know how many hours, and almost perished. They ran out of gas.

Seems to me they didn't take too great precaution with navigators when they were island hopping in those days.

Redman: You can't blame the Army too much, because up to that time, the Army had had practically no experience flying over water. They just hadn't had any. Up to the time of World War II, this is surprising as you look back. You look at life now days - the instrumental help that you have in a plane, landing in a fog, and so forth. It doesn't seem possible. The Army's experience in those days when they traveled from the East Coast to the West Coast was to follow the railroad tracks. That's the way they used to fly. When you come to sending them out over a wide wide ocean like the Pacific, they just didn't have the experience.

Then another thing, they didn't have the radio operators. That's another thing that they didn't seem to realize. You can't make a radio operator overnight. The expansion that took place was tremendous, particularly for the Army - Navy too, of course.

Of course, the Navy had had some experience. For instance - you fly from one place to another in the Pacific and you look for a little bit of an island.

Q: Pin-pointing something.

Redman: Pin-pointing, absolutely. As far as the expanses of the ocean is concerned, those little islands out there were like a couple of city blocks; that's all. So the Navy had this system - they did the best navigation they could. Dead reckoning, we call it. Plus sights, they carried a sexton and all that. They did the best they could. They estimated the sea, and the wind, and all these things. They put all those factors into their dead reckoning. When they arrived at a point where they should sight that little island, and they didn't sight it; they they would go into a prepared plan. Which involved the use of flying a square. The factors that they put in to the sides of the square were the visibility, the direction of the wind, and the sea and so forth. They would fly a square of a certain size. If they did not sight their objective the first go-round in that square - the square was small enough that you could see everything in the center of the square. After you flew the four sides of it, you enlarged. Then you flew four sides of a larger square. If they had gasoline, they never failed to find their objective.

Q: That was the technique of the rescue service too, wasn't it? But the question was the gasoline, when you were really going to the limit of your endurance in the first place.

Redman: Yes, sure, that's right. But so often the Army would fly until they thought they should have picked up their objective, and then they'd say to themselves, "We'll fly a little further." Often times they left it behind, or left it off to one side or the other.

Q: Guess work, under those circumstances, is not very good. Is it?

Redman: No.

Q: Were you with Admiral Nimitz up to the signing of the treaty for peace?

Redman: No. I left the staff in March 1945. I'd been trying to break away from the staff for some time. It's an old adage, custom, practice in the Navy that a Naval Officer's got to have a big ship command - at least it was at that time.

Q: Otherwise, he doesn't make flag?

Redman: Otherwise, he doesn't get selected. The war was running out, without me ever getting a big ship, and I wanted wartime experience. I filed a couple of formal requests for sea duty addressed to the Bureau of Personnel which required the endorsement of my boss.

Q: Was Admiral Nimitz endorsing these?

Redman: You are asking a very embarrassing question, because my requests were tucked away in my Chief of Staff's desk.

Q: It was a wartime service. You were filling a billet and doing it well.

Redman: Finally I got ordered to Washington to the Bureau, because I wanted to get out of there. I finally got them stirred up to the point that they decided to find me a relief.

There were a couple of possibilities, but the one that was selected was then in command of one of the big battleships. He wasn't too happy either getting pulled off of it. In those days, the Captains were lucky if they could keep a ship more than five or six months. So, he'd had it long enough. He finally came and relieved me, and I was allowed to go.

I was skipper of the MASSACHUSETTS. I found her out at Ulithi. I had her during what they called the last two operations. Both of them were off Okinawa, or in that area. I had her through that. At the end of the war, I was given six other ships, and made a Task Group Commander in charge of them.

We started off the day after the treaty was signed. We were part of the fleet that was standing by outside Tokyo Bay. Immediately after the Treaty was signed, I took these other six ships - I had two different size carriers, two different size cruisers, two different destroyers, in addition to my own ship - and brought them home. I took two to Bremerton, and sent the other four down the coast.

Q: Admiral tell me more about your relationship with Admiral Nimitz as the war came to an end, or after the war when you had retired, or when he had retired.

Redman: After I left the staff, and went to command the MASSACHUSETTS, I didn't see the Admiral again until after the war.

I became the Commandant of the 12th Naval District, with headquarters here in San Francisco. The Admiral was living in Berkeley at that time. I renewed my acquaintance with him, and also became acquainted with Mrs. Nimitz more so than ever before. I had met her before. We got to know them very well. We were greatly honored when on occasion we were invited up to their home.

Q: A beautiful place, wasn't it? That garden was terrific.

Redman: Yes. The Admiral served the drinks, and Mrs. Nimitz cooked and served the dinner. It was a foursome. That was really quite an honor.

As Commandant, I was kind of his logistic support, you might say, in the old Federal Office Building in San Francisco. He had an office right above mine. He used it only infrequently.

One of the things about Admiral Nimitz' character that was in my mind that is worthwhile to the biographer, was that the Admiral never felt that he should impose upon the organization any more than was absolutely necessary. Of course, as you may suspect he had a great deal of fan mail - post war - for a long time. It took a long period of time before it dwindled.

Q: He was actually, by law, on active duty, wasn't he?

Redman: By law, he was on active duty for the rest of his life. He could have had a very large staff as General Mac Arthur had. He choose, as one of those five-star heroes, to have only at first a Lieutenant, junior grade who was an ex-Chief Yeoman in the Navy; a civil service secretary, a girl; and a Marine Sergeant driver. He handled his own fan mail with that small organization for quite a while. Then he gave up the Lieutenant, junior grade and the civil service secretary. He said at that time if he needed any secretarial assistance or otherwise, he would depend upon the Commandant of the 12th Naval District to help him. But he kept his Marine driver. The Marine driver that he had still lives here in town.

Has Mrs. Nimitz mentioned in any of her conversations about the ex-Marine Sergeant named Cozard?

Q: No, but she's been lamenting the fact that just the other day Caldwell called on her. He's going back to Vietnam. He was one of the Marines. He was the last one the Admiral had, and they were very fond of him. But she hasn't mentioned Cozard.

Redman: Cozard was very close to the Admiral and Mrs. Nimitz. I'm sure that she just hasn't thought of Cozard.

Q: She probably hasn't because when I met the Admiral in '62 the Marine he had was about to be relieved by this Caldwell who continued with him until his death. They were both there simultaneously when I met him.

Redman: I didn't know those two. Cozard is right here in San Francisco. He works for the Pacific Gas and Electric Company. He's kind of an assistant to Bob Gros who is the Vice President of Public Relations for PG&E.

Nobody was closer during those years as far as personal experiences and those kind of things are concerned than Cozard was. He took the Admiral every place.

Q: She just hasn't thought about him.

Redman: Probably not. I would see him from time to time and we would see them socially over those years. We felt very close to them. They knew my first wife, and they liked her very well. I lost her with cancer in 1955, and then I married this girl.

They've been very fond of her, and we'd see them from time to time. As a matter of fact, we were one of the fewpeople who were allowed to go up and see the Admiral when he was pretty sick, and it wasn't long before he was gone. Mrs. Nimitz took us upstairs in the quarters to see him. I think he was watching the Army-Navy football game that year. I can't remember just when the Admiral died.

Q: He died in February.

Mrs. Redman: It was New Years' Day that we last saw him. He and Catherine were watching one of the New Year's bowl games, not the Army-Navy Game.

Q: That was less than two months before he died. He wasn't at home then?

Mrs. Redman: Yes, he was at home. We had gone to a brunch that Jack and Amelia Taylor gave down at the Casa de la Vista - the annex to the Officer's Club down on the waterfront at Treasure Island. When we left, we thought we'd drop by the Nimitz's quarters on Yerba Buena Island. I don't think the Admiral had been home from the hospital too long then. Mrs. Nimitz greeted us, and we asked her if she thought it would be all right for us to see the Admiral as we knew he hadn't been seeing many people. She said she thought it would cheer him up and urged us to come upstairs, but suggested we only stay about 15 minutes so as not to tire him. He looked rather thin and weak, but seemed genuinely pleased to see us. We had a glass of sherry with them. Although it was an effort for him to speak very much, he said when the sherry was served, "Jack, you can have something stronger if you like."

I just ran across this picture of him - you've seen that one of him?

Q: Excellent picture. Yes, I have seen it.

Redman: We've got several other of the Admiral, but we like that one of him.

Q: It's a natural one.

Redman: We asked him to autograph it.

Q: Tell me about Admiral Nimitz's sense of humor. He did have a well-developed one, an unpredictable one.

Redman: Oh, yes, he loved stories. I can tell you about one occasion. It was at a banquet at the St. Francis Hotel, about 300 people there. I think it was along about the time that I was a Commandant in 1955, or 1956.

It was supposed to be stag. He sat at a high table, the dais was up high. He sat back, and the table was out in front of him in such a way that he really didn't take in the part of the gathering that was just below the table. He loved to tell, for men only, some very fine stories that you might say were a little bit off color. He got up, and I knew that he would have a few of his regular good stories to tell. He stood up, and as he did so, he looked down at the tables that were close in below the dais, and discovered about six or eight women reporters sitting at several press tables down there. He took a great big deep breath, and went ahead and told his stories anyway. I could see that he made up his mind that if they came to report one of his affairs, they could just take it.

Q: It wasn't a matter of sex under those circumstances. They were there for business.

Redman: That's right. And he had some wonderful stories to tell. I could tell one of his stories --- Does it make any difference?

Q: No.

Redman: One of his stories that I always remember, and I've gotten quite a bit of mileage out of is -- A story that he tells of his relationship with General Omar Bradley after the war.

It was following General Bradley's tour as head of the Veterans Administration. They had been old friends for years. He was asking General Bradley about some of his experiences in handling the veterans problems in the Administration. General Bradley told him this story about how beset they were after the war by the G.I.s who wanted to know what their rights were, and arrange for thier education in accordance with this new Bill of Rights which had been enacted. So, they had drafted some of their lesser lights from up in the top floors who were used to doing nothing but filing and things like that, to get down to the lobby and man these desks to provide information to these G.I.s when they would come in.

There was this old codger who was delighted with his new role in life, and he had a desk down there, and he was looking for business. He saw a young fellow who was an obvious G.I., who kept wandering around. He said, "Young man, can I do something for you?" This young G.I. said, "Yes, you can. I came in to find out about this Bill of Rights. I want to find out what I can get out of it." This old codger said, "What are you interested in, education?" The G.I. said, "Yes, that's the thing I'm really interested in. I'd like to go to college." The old codger said, "Fine, fine. What do you want to learn?" The G.I. said, "I thought I'd like to be trained to be a midwife." The old codger said, "Wait a minute, young fellow. A midwife is a woman." The G.I. said, "Yes, ordinarily conceived as such. Look, you have male doctors, and you have female doctors. You have male nurses, and female nurses. You have female midwives.

Why can't you have a male midwife?" The old guy scratched his head, and said, "Now wait a minute, I'll have to look into this. Could you come back tomorrow?" The G.I. said, "Yes, sure, I'll be back tomorrow."

So, he came back the next day. The old codger greeted him with open arms, and said, "I've got just the thing for you. There's a little college down south that's just perfect for what you want." So, he lined him all up, signed on the line and everything, and arranged for him to get his money and those kind of things. He got him off on this little trip down to this little college. The G.I. went down there, and he took this course. Finally he came up with a diploma as a midwife. He went back to his little home town which wasn't too far away. He rented a little office, and he bought a black bag with instruments, and sat down and waited for business. He hung a shingle out.

He sat around there for about a week. Finally, there was a patter of footsteps running down the hall, the door burst open, and this farmer-type individual came in. He said, "I'm looking for the midwife." The G.I. very modestly said, "I'm the midwife." Then there was the to-do about reading the diploma and all that. Finally the farmer said, "You'll have to do because our only doctor has gone about 90 miles away. You'll have to take care of it."

They ran out and jumped into a car, and went to the farm. The G.I. took off his coat, and put on his white jacket. He said to the husband, "You just sit down in here and read a magazine. Don't you worry. I'll take care of everything." He sat down in the living room. The G.I. went in the bedroom and closed the door, and took his black bag with him.

He was in there about 10 minutes, and he came and cracked the door, and said to the husband, "Say, I wonder if you've got a screw driver - blade about six inches long and a quarter of an inch wide, something like that." The husband said, "Yes, I've got a tool chest down below mister. I'll go down and get one." So, he came up and knocked on the door. The G.I. said, "Fine, just I need. Now you go back to your magazine and don't you worry. Everything's going to be fine."

About 20 minutes went by, and the G.I. cracked the door again. He said to the husband, "I wonder if you might not have a putty knife." The husband said, "Gee, mister, I've never done any of that kind of work - a glazer, you call it, don't you? I've got a neighbor lives nearby. He did some of that kind of work last winter. Maybe he's got one." He said, Run over and get it." So he ran over, got it, came back, and knocked on the door. The G.I. came to the door, and he said, "Just the thing, just the thing, fine. Now you just go back to your magazine, don't worry, everything's going to be fine."

In about another 20 minutes, the G.I. cracked the door again, and said, "Say, mister, I wonder if you'd have a piece of wire about five or six inches long - a good stiff piece of wire, with a hook in the end of it." The husband said, "I

no page numbered # 48.

haven't got anything like that around here. How would a coat hanger do?" The G.I. said, "Fine, a wire coat hanger, just what I need." He went and got the coat hanger, and knocked on the door. The G.I. said, "Fine, fine, now don't you worry, go and sit down."

The husband couldn't stand it any longer. He said, "Look here, what's going on? First you want a screw driver, then you want a putty knife, then you want a coat hanger. What's the matter? Aren't things going right? Are you having any trouble?" The G.I. said, "Trouble, hell, yes. I can't get the damm bag open!"

That's a sample of the kind of stories he told.

Q: Admiral, tell me about this incident that involved Cribbage with Admiral Nimitz.

Redman: I don't know whether I mentioned it before or not, but usually when I traveled with the Admiral and the doctor - except for the time that I mentioned when we went down to Guadalcanal - the other trips we flew in an Army Air Corps B-24. The Admiral used to love to play Cribbage, and I played with him on several occasions when there wasn't anything else to do.

Q: Was this simply an outlet for him?

Redman: Yes, he loved Cribbage. We used to play for 25¢ a game, and a penny a point.

I remember on one occasion when the Admiral wanted to go and see the results of the operation in Kwajalein. On this particular occasion it seemed best for us to take a B-24 out of Hickham Field, and fly down to Tarawa because they had by that time improved the air strip so that a B-24 could land. Then we took a Navy seaplane from there and flew up to Kwajalein and landed in the Kwajalein Island lagoon.

Kwajalein, as I recall, was stated to be the largest coral atoll in the world. To give you an idea of how large it was -- after we landed there, we took a destroyer that was inside this coral atoll lagoon. We traveled for over two hours inside the lagoon to go from the island of Kwajalein - which was at the lower part of the perimeter of an enormous coral reef; at the bottom of the lagoon was Kwajalein Island - up to Lemur where most of the Marine heavy fighting had taken place. It took about two hours on the destroyer going about ten knots.

Q: That was really the diameter.

Redman: Yes, it was really the diameter. I had just never seen anything like these coral reefs out there. It just didn't seem possible that these little coral bugs or whatever they are, could build anything like that over the years.

Q: Think of the amount of time involved in it.

Redman: To get back to the Cribbage. On the B-24 - I think we flew by night from Hickman Field down to the island of Tarawa --

Q: That was even more hazardous, wasn't it for the Admiral?

Redman: Hazardous, how do you mean?

Q: In case you had to come down.

Redman: If you go out over the water in a land plane, it doesn't make much difference whether you come down in the daylight or come down at night. You can, maybe, splash it down on occasion in a calm sea; but your chances of landing in the ocean with a land plane make the odds pretty slim.

I think it was a night flight. The Admiral loved to play Cribbage. I've always been a very poor gambler, if I thought the stakes would damage my finances; so to speak. In the case of the Admiral, because he loved Cribbage so much, and because I was his junior, and he was my superior - I didn't want to win. I wanted him to win, I wanted him to enjoy it. This particular night, try as I could, I couldn't lose. One game I double skunked him for $4.00 - that's 25¢ a game, a penny a point. The Admiral was a pretty good sport about it, but I think he was kind of shook up about it.

That night, when it got to be along about 11 o'clock, and we were going to land about 6 or 7 o'clock in the morning; and we about to turn in - the doctor had already gone to sleep - he kept looking for his bag and he couldn't find it. He knew it was in the plane some place.

He had a beautiful Cribbage board that had been made for him by the SeaBees out of lucite. That's that plexiglass material that they use in the nose of a plane. It was blue colored, tinged with blue. The SeaBees had done the most magnificent job on it. I must ask Mrs. Nimitz about that - if that board is still around. I'd like to see it again. Then, they had found a particular pouch that it would just fit into. They gave it to him as a present. He was very proud of it, because he was very proud of those SeaBees. He thought those SeaBees were a great organization. And they did do a magnificent job out there in the Pacific.

When we were ready to turn in, he kept looking for his bag and he couldn't find it. We never took off our clothes, there were no bunks. We'd just lie down, and snooze with some blankets. He said, "Here, put this in your bag. Give it back to me when we get home." We didn't have chance to play anymore during that trip. When we arrived back - I would have him to myself on these trips like that - there would be the

Chief of Staff, the Operations Officer, and everybody else on the staff would take him over -- so to pseak.

Q: See him no more for a little while?

Redman: I wouldn't see much of him, except on official matters for a while. When we arrived at his quarters, I lived right next door; I got out of one car, and he got out of a car right up in front of his quarters. He saw me getting out, and he called to me, and said, "Redman, send over my Cribbage board with your bill." I kept track of how much he owed me. I said, "Aye, aye sir," I just ruled out $6.25 or something like that, and tucked it in the top of this Cribbage board. I went over and gave it to the orderly who was outside who was the Admiral's aide.

Later on, down at the headquarters, his Marine orderly came and laid down this amount of money on my desk. I looked up at him, and I said, "What's that?" He said, "Admiral Nimitz told me to give this to you." I knew what it was, of course. I said, "Okay, thank you very much."

The night on the plane when I was putting away the Admiral' cribbage board he saw one of the hunting knives which had been issued to servicemen by Admiral Davis. This one had been issued down in San Diego. Davis was connected with the Amphibious Groups. I guess I had not quite as much right as the ordinary

G.I. did, but I still was flying around where I might be a survival man too. The Admiral saw this in my bag, and he said, "Where did you get that knife?" I said, "Admiral Davis gave it to me when I went to San Diego." He said, "Gee, that's a nice one." I said, "Would you like it, Admiral? There's plenty of them around, I'll get another one." "Oh, no," he said, "I wouldn't take yours."

So, I remembered that after the Marine had brought down the money for the Cribbage debt. I made some inquiry about them - where to get these hunting knives. They said you could buy them over in some place in Pearl Harbor. So, I sent over and got one. It didn't cost too much. It was a little bit different. You know how those things are - one manufacturer puts out one style, and another puts out another.

Q: Slightly different version, yes.

Redman: Yes. Later on in the day, he sent for me. So, I took the knives with me. After we discussed the official problem, I said, "Admiral, you admired that knife I had in my bag the other night. Here's two of them, and you can have either one. It doesn't make a bit of difference. There's no sentiment attached to mine, as far as I'm concerned." He said, "No, I wouldn't have yours. I'll take the other one." He said, "Where did you get this?" My hesitation was the thing that exposed me. He said,

"You bought it, didn't you?" I said, "But it didn't cost anything, Admiral. Please accept it from me." Then I made a terrible mistake. I said, "Anyway, I'll get it back at Cribbage." He said, "You get the hell out of my office." Of course, he wasn't angry at all.

INDEX

for an interview

with

VICE ADMIRAL JOHN ROLAND REDMAN, U. S. NAVY (RET.)

Aiea, 15

Annapolis, Md., 24

Army, 34-35

Aukland, 22-23

Berkeley, California, 39

Bowling, 15-16

Bradley, General Omar, 44-45

Caldwell, J. Emett, 40-41

Callaghan, Daniel Judson, 22, 30

Callaghan, Admiral William M., 30-32

Communications Volunteer Reserve, 1

Cozard, George E., 40-41

Cribbage, 52-55

Curts, Commander M. E., 4

Dead reckoning, 35-36

Espiritu Santo, 25-33

Exercise, 7-9, 15

FBI, 2

Fitch, RADM Aubrey W., 26

Ghormley, Admiral Robert Lee, 21-24

Guadalcanal, 11, 22, 25-26, 49

Guam, 6

Halsey, Admiral William Frederick, 23

Horseshoes, 6

Japanese, 11, 14, 26; codes, 4

Jondreau, Romeo Joseph, 12

Kailua, 7

Kimmel, Admiral Husband Edward, 4

King, Admiral Ernest J., 4

Kwajalein, 11, 13, 50

MacArthur, General Douglas, 40

Mariannas, 11

Maryland, 14

Massachusetts, 38-39

McMorris, Admiral Charles H., 9

Midway, Battle of, 4

Nimitz, Mrs. Chester W., 16, 39-43, 52

Noumea, 22

Oahu, 18

Ofstie, Ralph, 32-33

Okinawa, 38

Pearl Harbor, 5-6, 14, 17

Richardson, General Robert Charlwood, Jr., 18-20

Spruance, Admiral Raymond Ames, 7-10

Stories, 43-48

Tarawa, 11-14, 50-51

Taylor, Jack and Amelia, 42

Tennis, 9, 24

Tokyo Bay, 38

Treasure Island, 42

Twining, General Nate, 34

Ulithi, 38

Vandergrift, General A. A., 26, 29

Washington, D. C. 24

Weems, Captain V. P. H., 32

World War II, 2-32, 49-52; Treaty Signing, 37-38

www.ingramcontent.com/pod-product-compliance
Lightning Source LLC
Chambersburg PA
CBHW080620170426
43209CB00007B/1474